Michael Oakeshott

Series Introduction

The *Major Conservative and Libertarian Thinkers* series aims to show that there is a rigorous, scholarly tradition of social and political thought that may be broadly described as 'conservative', 'libertarian' or some combination of the two.

The series aims to show that conservatism is not simply a reaction against contemporary events, nor a privileging of intuitive thought over deductive reasoning; libertarianism is not simply an apology for unfettered capitalism or an attempt to justify a misguided atomistic concept of the individual. Rather, the thinkers in this series have developed coherent intellectual positions that are grounded in empirical reality and also founded upon serious philosophical reflection on the relationship between the individual and society, how the social institutions necessary for a free society are to be established and maintained, and the implications of the limits to human knowledge and certainty.

Each volume in the series presents a thinker's ideas in an accessible and cogent manner to provide an indispensable work for both students with varying degrees of familiarity with the topic as well as more advanced scholars.

The following twenty volumes that make up the entire *Major Conservative and Libertarian Thinkers* series are written by international scholars and experts.

The Salamanca School by Andre Azevedo Alves (LSE, UK) & Professor José Manuel Moreira (Porto, Portugal)
Thomas Hobbes by Dr R. E. R. Bunce (Cambridge, UK)
John Locke by Professor Eric Mack (Tulane, US)
David Hume by Professor Christopher J. Berry (Glasgow, UK)
Adam Smith by Professor James Otteson (Yeshiva, US)
Edmund Burke by Professor Dennis O'Keeffe (Buckingham, UK)
Alexis de Tocqueville by Dr Alan S Kahan (Paris, France)
Herbert Spencer by Alberto Mingardi (Istituto Bruno Leoni, Italy)
Ludwig von Mises by Richard Ebeling (Trinity College)

Joseph A. Schumpeter by Professor John Medearis (Riverside, California, US)
F. A. Hayek by Dr Adam Tebble (UCL, UK)
Michael Oakeshott by Dr Edmund Neill (Oxford, UK)
Karl Popper by Dr Phil Parvin (Cambridge, UK)
Ayn Rand by Professor Mimi Gladstein (Texas, US)
Milton Friedman by Dr William Ruger (Texas State, US)
James M. Buchanan by Dr John Meadowcroft (King's College London, UK)
The Modern Papacy by Dr Samuel Gregg (Acton Institute, US)
Robert Nozick by Ralf Bader (St Andrews, UK)
Russell Kirk by Jon Pafford
Murray Rothbard by Gerard Casey

Of course, in any series of this nature, choices have to be made as to which thinkers to include and which to leave out. Two of the thinkers in the series – F. A. Hayek and James M. Buchanan – have written explicit statements rejecting the label 'conservative'. Similarly, other thinkers, such as David Hume and Karl Popper, may be more accurately described as classical liberals than either conservatives or libertarians. But these thinkers have been included because a full appreciation of this particular tradition of thought would be impossible without their inclusion; conservative and libertarian thought cannot be fully understood without some knowledge of the intellectual contributions of Hume, Hayek, Popper and Buchanan, among others. While no list of conservative and libertarian thinkers can be perfect, then, it is hoped that the volumes in this series come as close as possible to providing a comprehensive account of the key contributors to this particular tradition.

John Meadowcroft
King's College London

Michael Oakeshott

Edmund Neill

Major Conservative and Libertarian Thinkers

Series Editor: John Meadowcroft

Volume 8

BLOOMSBURY
NEW YORK • LONDON • NEW DELHI • SYDNEY

Bloomsbury Academic
An imprint of Bloomsbury Publishing Plc

175 Fifth Avenue	50 Bedford Square
New York	London
NY 10010	WC1B 3DP
USA	UK

www.bloomsbury.com

Hardback edition first published in 2011 by the Continuum International Publishing Group Inc.
This paperback edition published by Bloomsbury Academic 2013

© Edmund Neill, 2013

All rights reserved. No part of this publication may be reproduced or transmitted in any form or by any means, electronic or mechanical, including photocopying, recording, or any information storage or retrieval system, without prior permission in writing from the publishers.

No responsibility for loss caused to any individual or organization acting on or refraining from action as a result of the material in this publication can be accepted by Bloomsbury Academic or the author.

Library of Congress Cataloging-in-Publication Data
A catalog record for this book is available from the Library of Congress.

ISBN: HB: 978-0-8264-2178-4
PB: 978-1-4411-4132-3

Typeset by Deanta Global Publishing Services, Chennai, India

Contents

Series Editor's Preface ix

1 **Michael Oakeshott's Life** 1
2 **Michael Oakeshott as Defender of Pluralism and Modernity** 11
   Idealism, the Early Writings and *Experience and Its Modes* 17
   Politics, Rationalism and the Conversation of Mankind 31
   Oakeshott's Late Work: *On Human Conduct* and *On History* 51
      On the theoretical understanding of *On Human Conduct* 52
      The civil condition 61
      On History 69
   Conclusion 77
3 **The Reception of Michael Oakeshott's Thought** 79
4 **Oakeshott's Continuing Relevance: Some Meditations on Conservatism and Liberalism** 98

Notes 115
Bibliography 129
Index 139

Series Editor's Preface

Michael Oakeshott was one of the principal political philosophers of the twentieth century. His work emphasizes the importance of tradition as well as practical knowledge and experience to civil society and political life. This has led him to be frequently interpreted as a conservative opponent of modernity. But his work also recognizes the pluralism and diversity inherent to in contemporary societies and the consequent need for the state to be organized as a somewhat loose 'civil association' that does not pursue a particular conception of the common good that would inevitably privilege of one group's values over others. This aspect of Oakeshott's work can lead to a reading that places him within the liberal or libertarian tradition.

Oakeshott, then, is a complex and challenging thinker whose work taken as a whole defies simple categorization or easy interpretation. Indeed, of all the thinkers collected in this series, Oakeshott could well be described as the most 'difficult'. Given this, Dr Edmund Neill of Oxford University has done a remarkable job in presenting Oakeshott's work in such a coherent and cogent manner. Neill provides a reliable and accessible account of Oakeshott's thought that demonstrates remarkable insight in synthesising the different aspects of his work into a cohesive whole. Readers of this volume will be left in no doubt that time invested in navigating Oakeshott's thought is time very well spent.

I am confident that this excellent volume will prove indispensable to those unfamiliar with Oakeshott's work, such as students encountering him for the first time, as well as more advanced scholars of political and social thought. As such, this volume makes a crucial contribution to the Major Conservative and Libertarian Thinkers series.

John Meadowcroft
King's College London

Chapter 1

Michael Oakeshott's Life

At the time of his death in 1990, Michael Oakeshott had at best an ambiguous status, even amongst the educated public. For some, he seemed to be the quintessential Tory philosopher in person, the man who had symbolically ended the Attlee government's intellectual hegemony when he replaced Harold Laski as Professor of Political Science at the London School of Economics in 1951, had (along with Friedrich Hayek) undermined the intellectual plausibility of post-war planning and had even provided Margaret Thatcher with a political philosophy. Thus for Richard Crossman, the Labour MP and former Oxford philosophy fellow, he was a 'cavalier iconoclast' who was intent upon destroying the school 'dedicated by the Webbs to the scientific study of the improvement of human society' (Crossman 1951: 60–1); for Ernest Gellner, he was best described as someone who 'damned egalitarian and welfare do-gooding' (Gellner 1995: 3) and for *The Times*'s obituary writer, although he had had no direct influence on her, he 'more than anybody else . . . [had] articulated the real philosophical foundations' of Thatcherite policies (*The Times* 1990: 11). For others, even more negatively, the logical implication of Oakeshott's arguments seemed to be to eliminate the very possibility of political philosophizing altogether, so that one was either entirely at the mercy of whichever tradition one found oneself located, or, alternatively, simply proceeded on a whim. Thus for Crossman, Oakeshott was guilty of heaping 'contempt and ridicule on Utopians and sentimentalists who believe that the individual can transcend his tradition and that principles are worth fighting for' (Crossman 1951: 60–1), something which the renowned political academic Bernard Crick thought should ultimately be put down to Oakeshott's personality – he was, for Crick, a 'sceptical, polemical, paradoxical, gay and bitter spirit', a 'lonely nihilist' (Crick 1963: 65). A little more positively, some of the academic community regarded Oakeshott respectfully, if somewhat warily, as advocating a particular view of studying politics which stressed the virtues of a particular version of political theorizing, one that deliberately shunned the possibility of quantitative scientific predictions, but also stressed the value of a certain kind of historical investigation of political texts. Unsurprisingly, such an approach tended to appeal to those of a generally conservative disposition, such as Noel O'Sullivan, Nevil Johnson and Kenneth Minogue, but Oakeshott's work had also appealed more widely to those who sought to uphold the value of history in political investigation. Nevertheless before 1990, only one book on Oakeshott had appeared (Greenleaf 1966), and it is only since his death that Oakeshott's work has begun to receive the kind of detailed attention it deserves, though many questions concerning it remain – hence the continuing need for such a book as this. Before going on to examine Oakeshott's work in detail in the remaining chapters, however, let us briefly examine the nature of Oakeshott's life and career.

The second of three brothers, Oakeshott was born in 1901 into a household that was not wealthy, but one which strongly valued education and had a definite interest in politics and culture. His father, the son of a Newcastle postmaster, was a civil servant working for the Inland Revenue at Somerset House. A Fabian socialist, he was a friend of George Bernard Shaw, and wrote a Fabian pamphlet on the reform of the Poor Law and supported granting votes for women, though he disapproved of the more militant tactics of the suffragettes. Nevertheless, as Oakeshott himself stressed, his father took his role as a non-party civil servant very seriously, even to the extent of not enforcing his political views on his children – he was, Oakeshott declared, 'never a party man, any more than I am', and 'his interests were always more literary than political' (cited in Grant 1990: 12). He was also an agnostic, in contrast to Oakeshott's mother, who was the daughter of a London vicar and worked as a nurse. A woman who took a lifelong interest in doing charitable work, she met Oakeshott's father at the Hoxton Settlement, and later became involved with the Children's Country Holiday Fund, but it was arguably her religious faith that was most important to Oakeshott. Never doctrinally orthodox, religion was something that remained of considerable significance to him throughout his life, as his lyrical description of religion in *On Human Conduct* makes clear (Oakeshott 1975: 81–6). Equally, Oakeshott's religious interests were mediated by a lifelong interest in the work of the French essayist and sceptic, Michel de Montaigne, and this was a passion that he inherited from his father. So although it was only later that Oakeshott developed the arguments that made him famous, he nevertheless owed significant intellectual debts to his parents.

However, although the influence of his parents was important to him, arguably the education that Oakeshott received both at school and university was even more significant in his development. Rather than attending a traditional grammar school, let alone a well-known public school, Oakeshott went to St George's, Harpenden, an innovative coeducational school which encouraged in Oakeshott a certain nonconformity and bohemianism, which remained throughout his life – though it should be mentioned that he was conventional enough to become Captain of the School. At the heart of the school was its headmaster, the Reverend Cecil Grant, who was a theologian, a socialist, enthusiastic about Pre-Raphaelite art, and a friend of the famous educational reformer, Maria Montessori. Liable to start explaining Kant's categorical imperative and Hegelian metaphysics to fifteen-year-old boys at the least provocation, he was nevertheless remembered by Oakeshott as a 'remarkably "undominating"' personality who sought to impart a 'style of life, rather than a doctrine' (Grant 1990: 119), and who eschewed intellectualization as a value, preferring to let his pupils roam relatively wild to develop themselves as individuals. (As will become clear in subsequent chapters, these were all values that were to be highly significant ones for Oakeshott later – Oakeshott was a determined believer in the importance of practical knowledge, individuality and the plurality of intellectual disciplines.) Subsequently, at Cambridge University, Oakeshott read history as a scholar at Gonville and Caius College, Cambridge, going up in 1920, narrowly missing having to serve in the First World War. There he read such classic historical authors as Maitland, Stubbs, Dicey, Acton and Ranke (O'Sullivan 2003: 31), but also took options in the history of political thought in both parts of the Tripos, and attended an 'Introduction to Philosophy' course taken by one of the last great Idealist thinkers, J. M. E. McTaggart. Still famous for his arguments concerning the nature of time, McTaggart argued that philosophy was something that aimed at the 'systematic study of the ultimate nature of reality', questioning premises that other disciplines – such as 'theology' and 'science' – regard as ultimate (McTaggart 1934: 183). (Once again this theme was one that remained important for Oakeshott throughout his life, as we shall subsequently discover.) Having graduated from Cambridge, Oakeshott took the opportunity to pursue his theological interests further, by visiting various important German universities in the 1920s, notably Tubingen and Marburg (where it is possible he may have heard Heidegger lecture – though there is no real direct evidence of this). And as well as reading a wide range of theological literature while in Germany, Oakeshott also took the opportunity to immerse himself in Holderlin, Nietzsche and Burckhardt, tastes that are apparent in his early essays, but which remain as an important subterranean influence throughout his life.

After a short period teaching English literature at King Edward VII grammar school at Lytham St Anne's in Lancashire, Oakeshott returned to Gonville and Caius College as a history fellow in 1927. There he taught a great deal of history to undergraduates, but his writings tended to focus on rather more abstract questions – examining the relationship between philosophy, religion and poetry in particular (see Oakeshott 1993). Of particular significance is the 'Essay on the Relations of Philosophy, Poetry, and Reality', which Oakeshott may have written to gain his MA, which was formally awarded in 1927 (O'Sullivan 2003: 39; Oakeshott 2004: 67–115). This essay identifies philosophy, as McTaggart had done, as the search – through questioning – for ultimate foundations, but also claims that poetry (by which Oakeshott essentially means 'rational intuition') can be a more direct route to ultimate reality, a position Oakeshott completely abandons later. So whilst it can be useful to look for early precursors for his later ideas, it is also important not to try and locate all of

Oakeshott's mature work in the writings of the 1920s: some of his early opinions were later completely abandoned. Arguably only with the publication of his first book, the well-known – if initially unfashionable – *Experience and Its Modes* in 1933 (Oakeshott 1933), did Oakeshott attain his maturity. An assured and sparkling work, this, as we will see in the next chapter, was importantly inspired by the Idealist F. H. Bradley amongst others, and also to some extent recalls the latter's coruscating prose style.

If *Experience and Its Modes* was at least greeted with a certain grudging respect in the 1930s – although it was utterly out of temper with the largely positivist type of philosophy being propagated at that time by professional philosophers – then Oakeshott's publication of a book concerning horse-racing in that decade encouraged a certain amount of sneering. *A Guide to the Classics, or How to Pick the Derby Winner* (Oakeshott and Griffith: 1936) seemed to provide ammunition for those who claimed that Oakeshott lacked intellectual seriousness, since being so 'frivolous' in an era when democratic regimes – and most notably Spain – were collapsing across Europe, seemed reprehensible. But the charge is at least partly an unfair one. For not merely did Oakeshott undertake to edit an – admittedly equivocal – anthology on *The Social and Political Doctrines of Contemporary Europe* (Oakeshott 1939) to which he added an interesting and perceptive introduction, he also undertook to fight in the Second World War, joining up in 1940. Eventually promoted to command a squadron of the GHQ Liaison Regiment, known as 'Phantom', Oakeshott apparently impressed his fellow officers with his quiet efficiency and lack of pretension (Grant 1990: 16). Despite his relative enjoyment of military life, however, Oakeshott returned to Cambridge with a firm and settled view that the procedures in wartime offered little help if one sought a guide as to how to behave in peacetime, in contrast to many other post-war intellectuals, perhaps most notably Karl Mannheim. And although this was not especially his motive for helping to set up a monthly journal with some of his Cambridge colleagues to explore politics and letters in 1947, namely the *Cambridge Journal*, nevertheless it was in this context that Oakeshott published his famous polemical essays aimed against collectivism and rationalism more generally – most notably 'Rationalism in Politics' and 'The Tower of Babel' – for which he continues to be best known.

It was with this reputation, therefore, that, after an unlikely year's appointment at the 'rationalist' and technocratic Nuffield College, Oxford, Oakeshott ended up with an even more unlikely appointment as the Professor of Political Science at the London School of Economics in 1951. For in contrast with his left-leaning 'activist' predecessors, Graham Wallas and Harold Laski, Oakeshott not only seemed to have little interest in influencing politics in practice, at that time he also seemed to be arguing that it was illegitimate for political theorists even to try to do so. Notoriously he claimed in his inaugural lecture, 'Political Education' that in politics 'men sail a boundless and a bottomless sea; there is neither harbour for shelter nor floor for anchorage, neither startingplace nor appointed destination', where the aim of the exercise was simply to 'keep afloat on an even keel' rather than to get anywhere in particular (Oakeshott 1991: 60). Unsurprisingly therefore, when not displaying overt irritation, contemporary political theorists and others working in political studies often tended to treat his work as a challenge to be overcome, a justification for tradition for tradition's sake, rather than as something particularly stimulating. Arguably they should not have treated Oakeshott's work in this way, as I suggest in Chapter 3, but given Oakeshott's reticence in debate and lack of proper footnoting, a certain bafflement was quite understandable. (Readers will have to decide for themselves whether they find Oakeshott's habit of quoting poetry without a proper reference – such as Matthew Arnold in *On Human Conduct* [Oakeshott 1975: 23] – a charming eccentricity or merely annoying.)

During his tenure as Professor of Political Science, Oakeshott published nothing other than a collected version of his essays from the 1940s and 1950s called *Rationalism in Politics and Other Essays* in 1962 (Oakeshott 1991) – though the lectures he gave at Harvard in 1958 were posthumously published as *Morality and Politics in Modern Europe* (Oakeshott 1993a) – but he was actively involved in the life of the School through his teaching. As well as being an astute and conscientious doctoral supervisor, as Russell Price in particular has memorably recorded (Price 1991), Oakeshott also had an important impact at the School on both undergraduates and postgraduate students. For undergraduates, there were his lectures on 'The History of Political Thought from the Ancient Greeks to the Present Day', (Oakeshott 1960s), which devoted considerable time to Plato, Aristotle, Roman political thought and medieval political experiences, before turning to more modern topics, and for postgraduate students there was Oakeshott's famous seminar on the history of political thought (Minogue 1991). Set up around 1960, in response to a central fiat from the University of London, Oakeshott established a one-year MSc concentrating on the history of political thought, and a key part of this course was a stimulating (if challenging) seminar in which classic texts in the history of political thought and prominent methods used to study it were extensively discussed. Participants at this seminar included such LSE luminaries as Elie Kedourie, Kenneth Minogue, John Charvet, Shirley Robin Letwin and Maurice Cranston, while an important legacy of the seminar was its influence on the nature of the academic careers of some of the younger participants. But arguably of even more importance was the contribution of this seminar in helping to crystallize Oakeshott's own ideas about the nature of historical study, the fruits of which were finally published as *On History and Other Essays* (Oakeshott 1983). This was after Oakeshott stopped contributing to the seminar in 1980–81, and long after his retirement in 1967.

Indeed, without the works Oakeshott produced after his retirement, his oeuvre would be much the poorer, since not only did he write *On History* in his later years, he then also produced the work that is now generally regarded as his magnum opus, *On Human Conduct* (1975). Like *On History*, this is a much tougher read than the essays collected in *Rationalism in Politics*, but as we shall see, it is also arguably a much more systematic work. Causing him much time and trouble to write, Oakeshott aimed to iron out some of the earlier ambiguities in his work, and, though the continual neologisms and use of Latin terminology may strike some as excessive, commentators have increasingly recognized that this is a work to be taken seriously. Finally, however, on a more personal level, despite the austerity of his last works, it should not be thought that Oakeshott's later years lacked enjoyment. Married three times, and by almost universal acclaim charming company, Oakeshott enjoyed an uncomplicated last few years in a largely unmodernized cottage in the village of Acton, Dorset, devoting himself to rereading some of his favourite authors, including St Augustine and Montaigne, 'the two most remarkable men who have ever lived' (Riley 1991: 113), and the joys of intelligent conversation. Never one for public honours, he remained genuinely unpretentious to the last, and continued to take delight in the pleasures offered by the immediate world around him. For although best known as a political philosopher, what ultimately becomes apparent about Oakeshott is how limited he regards this as a form of activity, and conversely the pleasure he took in the other experiences that life offered him – hearing Caruso sing before the First World War, bicycling through the Dutch countryside at the end of the Second World War, hearing philosophy lectures in 1920s Germany and strolling through Siena, his favourite Italian city (Riley 1991: 113). A man with a sharp and perceptive mind, his way of dealing with the world was deceptively simple, and it is no surprise to learn that he was not easily identified as a professional political philosopher when not in a university environment. That said, however, it is now time for us to examine his work.

Chapter 2

Michael Oakeshott as Defender of Pluralism and Modernity

In the first chapter, we briefly examined the nature of Oakeshott's life and career. Having done so, we can now proceed to consider the way in which his ideas evolved over the course of the twentieth century, through an examination of both his published and unpublished works. In many ways, however, this is not an easy task, despite the fact that Oakeshott has long been recognized as a notable figure in a number of important, related intellectual fields, including the history of ideas, the philosophy of history and – especially – in political philosophy. For although widely regarded as one of the most significant political theorists of the 1950s and 1960s when the discipline was widely believed to be in crisis (or even 'dead'),[1] lauded as one of the most important post-war philosophers of history working in an Anglo-American context (along with R. G. Collingwood)[2] and noted for his distinctive take on the gradual rise of individualism in Western European Europe, (see O'Sullivan 2000) getting to grips with the full range of Oakeshott's ideas has historically proved a highly challenging assignment for scholars and commentators. Indeed, Oakeshott has until recently often been labelled as a thinker *sui generis*, difficult to classify and come to terms with, and even sometimes dismissed as an uncompromising eccentric. Why is this?

Arguably two main factors have contributed to this state of affairs. First, Oakeshott's philosophical position has always seemed – certainly in the 1950s and 1960s, but also more recently – somewhat remote from those of his contemporaries. Thus in the post-war decades, when many philosophers, under the influence of such positivists as A. J. Ayer and T. D. Weldon, were insisting (to a greater or lesser extent) that the only way to obtain genuine knowledge in the humanities, just as much as the natural sciences, was to formulate and test hypotheses that were empirically verifiable (Ayer 1936; Weldon 1953) (or at least falsifiable),[3] and hence that one should concentrate on analysing the external aspects of human conduct – since these could be observed and tested – Oakeshott was pursuing a very different path. For although Oakeshott certainly conceded that such an approach to understanding human behaviour was a possible one, he also insisted that this does not exclude the possibility of using forms of understanding (such as 'History' and 'Practice') that regard agents' own self-understandings as crucially important when trying to explain their actions – hence denying the idea there is only one legitimate way to interpret human actions. Furthermore, although some of his contemporaries, notably Michael Polanyi and Gilbert Ryle, concurred with Oakeshott's strong insistence that all human activities require knowledge that can only be learned in practice, rather than simply that which can be explicitly formulated, against the grain of positivist orthodoxy (Polanyi 1958; Ryle 1949), Oakeshott went further than most in arguing that the denial of practical knowledge was traceable back to a certain kind of Enlightenment rationalism, originating with Bacon and Descartes. And equally, later in his career, whilst the advent of a philosophical climate in the 1970s and 1980s in Britain and America that took hermeneutics and pragmatism much more seriously – and was hence far less inclined to see the human sciences as merely inferior versions of the natural ones – certainly provided a much more promising environment for Oakeshott's work to get a fair hearing,[4] nevertheless his position remained at some distance from what was philosophically orthodox. In particular, his continued insistence that different ways of analysing human conduct are utterly incommensurable with one another, and that there is a more or less absolute distinction between philosophy and practice left him some way from the philosophical mainstream, which increasingly tended to stress the irreducibly practical nature of all forms of theoretical understanding. Likewise, as a political philosopher, Oakeshott's denial of both the possibility of any kind of genuine rational 'consensus' (even of the minimal 'overlapping' kind advocated by John Rawls),[5] or of there being any kind of genuinely substantive 'community' values within society has made him an uncomfortable thinker for both 'liberals' and 'communitarians' alike to recruit; overall Oakeshott remains a difficult thinker to place.

Second, and perhaps most crucially, until recently the general impression that Oakeshott's work gave was that it lacked any genuine unity, and instead consisted of a set of meditations on largely discrete topics. This tendency was at least partly encouraged by Oakeshott himself, since the major works he allowed to be published in his lifetime seemed designed to tackle quite separate questions. Thus *Experience and Its Modes* (1933) sought to argue in Idealist fashion that only philosophy, or 'experience without presupposition, reservation, arrest or modification' (Oakeshott 1933: 2)[6] was fully coherent and satisfactory, whilst acknowledging that certain incomplete ways (or 'modes') or apprehending experience were nevertheless more developed than others, these being 'Science', 'History' and 'Practice', 'politics' as such rarely being mentioned at all. By contrast, *Rationalism in Politics* (1962) seemed a far more overtly political work, intent on upholding the virtues of 'tradition', both epistemologically and morally, but considerably less keen (overtly at least) on arguing that 'Philosophy' can provide knowledge that is superior to those of the 'modes'. Equally *On Human Conduct* (1975), whilst retaining themes familiar from previous works, had a different focus again, exploring the idea of 'civil association' – a form of government Oakeshott regarded as appropriate for modern individuals, since (he claimed) it existed purely to guarantee their freedom, rather than for any extrinsic purpose, while the last major work published in his lifetime – *On History* (1983) – sought to codify Oakeshott's position on the philosophy of history, a subject that had preoccupied him throughout his long career.

In these circumstances, it is not surprising that commentators have historically struggled to find a 'guiding thread' that links all the themes in Oakeshott's published work together. Indeed for a long time Oakeshott scholars tended to eschew such a task altogether, instead preferring to undertake the more modest project of examining individual aspects of his work in article-length studies, trying to assess both the degree to which his views on a particular topic remained constant, and how sustainable his views were. In particular they tended to concentrate on exploring whether he was best described as a 'conservative' (for which, see Koerner 1985: 270–308; Pitkin 1973) or a 'liberal' (for which see Franco 1990a; Coats 1985), whether his philosophy of history was really sustainable (see Meiland 1965; Rotenstreich 1976: 111–31; King 1983; Boucher 1984; Walsh 1968 and Dray 1968) and the degree to which the early Idealism of *Experience and Its Modes* remained important for understanding the later development of his thought (compare Boucher and Vincent 2000; Gerencser 2000). By contrast, books on Oakeshott's thought tended to be relatively few and far between before his death in 1990 (or soon afterwards), limiting themselves either to attempting to provide reasonably clear expositions of his thought (see, e.g. Greenleaf 1966; Franco 1990b; Grant 1990) or to trying to situate him intellectually by comparing him with 'other' conservative theorists such as Leo Strauss (Devigne 1994). To some extent this situation has altered in the more recent past, with the appearance in print of Oakeshott's previously unpublished or uncollected pieces, which has both led to scholars paying closer attention to aspects of his work that were previously neglected – such as his views on religion, aesthetics and the history of ideas (see, respectively: Worthington 2000; Worthington 1995; O'Sullivan 2003) – and to some attempts to grasp the nature of Oakeshott's thought as a whole, for example, by such authors as Terry Nardin, Efraim Podoksik and Roy Tseng amongst others (see Nardin, 2001; Podoksik 2003; Tseng 2003). Notably, however, these interpretations continue to disagree fairly radically with one another, with there being no consensus as to whether Oakeshott is best seen as a 'conservative' or a 'liberal', as being an upholder or a critic of 'modernity',[7] or even whether it is most fruitful to analyse him as political theorist or a 'pure' philosopher.[8] In short, the debate as to how best to pigeonhole Oakeshott remains largely unresolved, despite some very interesting and insightful recent work.

Given these radically conflicting interpretations, it is obviously impossible simply to give an uncontroversial exposition of Oakeshott's views – the differences between them are clearly too wide to reconcile easily, and the aspects of his *oeuvre* one chooses to highlight will obviously vary according to the view one takes of his work. Nevertheless in what follows I will aim to cover the main areas within Oakeshott's published and unpublished output, whilst also attempting to provide something of a unifying interpretation of his work. Building on Efraim Podoksik's excellent work,[9] whilst not downplaying his anxieties about the effects of the Enlightenment project on modern society, I maintain that Oakeshott tends to be a cautious but firm defender of modernity, both philosophically and politically, seeking to uphold a range of positions that are unconventional, but nevertheless firmly 'modernist' in orientation. Philosophically, I argue that, although resistant to the idea put forward by many modernists that natural science is some kind of model which other intellectual disciplines ought to follow, Oakeshott has little sympathy for the idea that the pre-modern (let alone pre-Platonic) era represented a 'golden age' when theoretical disciplines were ideally integrated both with practice and with each other. And equally, he has little time for 'post-modernist' claims that philosophy has no role in determining the legitimacy or otherwise of intellectual disciplines. On a more political level, despite his respect for the role of tradition, and his worries about some of the effects of Enlightenment rationalism, I argue that Oakeshott becomes an increasingly strong advocate of the strongly pluralist individualism that he believes characterizes modernity, and hence of the form of government he believes most respects it – namely the 'civil condition' – since, as far as possible, this does prescribe individuals' courses of action. Unlike either pre-modern morality, in other words, or its modern equivalent, 'the morality of the common good', Oakeshott argues, the morality of individualism does not pretend that individuals naturally have a common substantive purpose; conversely, however, unlike the post-modernists,

Oakeshott does not arbitrarily maintain that the pluralism inherent in modern society is so great that we can neither understand one another as being part of a common tradition, nor argue that the individual self must be seen as necessarily fragmented – for Oakeshott it remains, potentially at least, very much capable of unity. To make this case, I will divide the following into three sections, first examining Oakeshott's early work including *Experience and Its Modes*, which, despite its Idealism comes close to upholding the value of the modes for their own sake. In the second section, I consider Oakeshott's critique of rationalism, as put forward in *Rationalism in Politics*, stressing that Oakeshott's epistemological critique of Enlightenment rationalism soon mutates into being a critique of a certain kind of modern morality. In the third section, I examine Oakeshott's argument as to how we should theorize about practices in *On Human Conduct*, before examining his analysis of the 'civil condition' in that work, and briefly considering his philosophy of history, particularly as put forward in *On History*, since as well as simply being the mode of understanding he was arguably most interested in, it also reveals more detail about the way in which Oakeshott believes individual actions should be theorized about.

Idealism, the Early Writings and *Experience and Its Modes*

Let us begin by examining Oakeshott's early writings, focusing in particular on Oakeshott's first really significant piece of published work, namely *Experience and Its Modes*. To do this, it is necessary to set Oakeshott's early work in the context of the Idealist tradition, since although in some ways Oakeshott's arguments even in this period deviated somewhat from theirs, nevertheless such British Idealist thinkers as T. H. Green, F. H. Bradley and Bernard Bosanquet still exerted a strong influence on him. For despite the fact that there were some important differences between the Idealists themselves in the early twentieth century even within the British Idealist tradition, let alone if we include the Italian Idealists such as Croce and Gentile as well, nevertheless they were all committed, broadly speaking, to four central tenets, all of which had an important impact on Oakeshott's work in this period.[10]

First, all the Idealists based their position on a strong critique of empiricism, arguing that thinkers such as David Hume and J. S. Mill had presented a false picture of how we gain knowledge by arguing that it begins with individual sense-experiences, the 'impressions' of which are then transformed by the mind into 'universals', purely by means of 'association'. By contrast, the Idealists argued, to be able to experience at all, the mind necessarily has to play a more active role in the process, since it is impossible for us to understand even the most simple of experiences except by relating them to other experiences by means of thought – for them the very idea of having a simple 'unmediated' experience is just a myth.[11] Second, following on from this, the Idealists maintained that it cannot be said that any experience we have is simply wrong – since there is no external reality independent of mind for us to check the experience against. Rather, all we can do to make sense of it is to see how well it coheres with our previous experiences – although it is important to note that every new experience that we have will also have an impact on those that we have already experienced. So instead of the coherence of a new experience being judged simply by how formally consistent it is with our previous experiences, using a measure derived solely from those previous experiences, in other words, rather its coherence must be judged with reference to all the aspects of all the particular experiences, both formal and substantive, giving the same weight to those of the new experience as it does to those of the older ones.[12] In short the Idealists believe that there can be no adequate measure of the coherence of a particular set of experiences other than in the set of experiences themselves – any attempt to use an external standard to determine this will inevitably fail to respect all the substantive aspects of the particular experiences involved, and will hence automatically end in abstraction.[13] Third, therefore, the Idealists maintained, the only way in which we can have a completely truthful and satisfactory experience is if we aim to reconcile *all* experiences with one another, a goal that all the Idealists took as being possible, at least in principle. They are all therefore accurately described as 'monists', since they believed that all experience is essentially one interrelated unity, generally associating the search for such a final perfect unity with the activity of philosophizing[14] – although Bradley was a significant exception to this, arguing that although philosophical reflection could demonstrate the *necessity* of such absolute unity existing, it could never be identified with it, since it lacked the immediacy he believed necessary to make something truly real. For because thought is always 'about' something, he argues, it is always inherently relational – whereas perfectly coherent experience must be totally and genuinely unified.[15] Finally, by analogy, the Idealists also argued strongly that at a societal level, just as at an epistemological one, conceptualizing human agents primarily as separate individual units is a mistake, since a correctly designed whole will necessarily be more coherent than its individual parts. So although they differ, for example, over the degree to which the central state is the body that provides this coherence, as it does for Hegel, with Bosanquet in particular being strongly sceptical of this notion,[16] the Idealists in general are completely at one in seeing society in general as prior to the individual – he or she is, for them, not an isolated unit, but 'a child of his time' (Hegel 1952: 11).

In many ways, at this stage of his career, Oakeshott follows these arguments of the Idealists closely, although, before writing *Experience and Its Modes*, he tends to adopt different parts of their position rather haphazardly, exploring different aspects of the Idealists' arguments rather than producing a particularly coherent and settled position. Thus in an unpublished 1925 manuscript, 'A Discussion of Some Matters Preliminary to the Study of Political Philosophy', disputing individualist conceptions of political theory, Oakeshott argues in the most thoroughly Hegelian terms that not merely can individual citizens only realize themselves in the context of a society, but that they can only do so fully if they subordinate their desires to the superior rationality of the state (see Oakeshott 1925: 131 ff.); however the essay very much represents a sketch rather than a fully coherent Idealist argument. Equally, on a more philosophical level, in an 'An Essay on the Relations of Philosophy, Poetry and Reality', Oakeshott raises the possibility that poetry, rather than philosophy, may provide the most direct route to ultimate reality, a discussion that very much takes its cue from Bradley's worries that philosophy may not provide sufficient intimacy and immediacy for us to do this – but again the article very much reads as a discussion of various Idealist ideas, rather than as a settled doctrine. (Oakeshott 2004: 67–115). By contrast, in *Experience and Its Modes*, Oakeshott provides a much more systematic metaphysical argument that ostensibly follows the core tenets of Idealism closely – albeit one that now almost completely ignores the political side of its position. Thus, first, in common with other Idealists, he argues that there is no such thing as an immediate experience without thought, rebutting the empiricist account of experience by pungently arguing that even something as seemingly unmediated as pain 'is actually felt... by connexion with previous experience, recognized as different or similar either in kind or degree' (Oakeshott 1933: 26), so that 'there is never in experience... an original, distinguishable from... interpretation' (Oakeshott 1933: 31–2). Second, following on from this, he maintains that, since 'facts are never merely observed, remembered or combined; they are always made' (Oakeshott 1933: 42); it means that the only criterion we have to measure the truth of any experience is how well it coheres with others that we have had – so that 'experience is always a coherent world of ideas' (Oakeshott 1933: 46). Third, by extension, he argues that this means that the only experience that is truly coherent and complete is one that encompasses the whole of experience – anything less than this will be partial, unfinished and abstract. As Oakeshott puts it himself: 'reality is a coherent world of concrete ideas, that is of things. Consequently, it is ... a single system, and it is real only as a whole'(Oakeshott 1933: 58). And, finally, rejecting Bradley's worries about 'immediacy', Oakeshott identifies the search for absolute coherence with philosophizing, an activity where 'experience [is] sought and followed entirely for its own sake' (Oakeshott 1933: 82), which (he believes) requires its adherents to be both thoroughly self-conscious and self-critical since they are forever searching for a more and more coherent experience, constantly reviewing the progress previously made.

However, on closer examination, Oakeshott's argument is not as conventionally Idealist as it first appears, and the main reason for this is his attitude towards the methods we use to understand the world that fall short of absolute coherence, methods that Oakeshott labels 'modes'. Up to a point, even here Oakeshott follows the conventional Idealist line, in arguing that such modes can necessarily never achieve complete coherence, in that they rely on one or more unquestioned presuppositions (or 'postulates') which cannot be overcome without destroying the integrity of the mode in question, but that they are nevertheless relatively sophisticated attempts at understanding experience, whose conclusions cannot be easily dismissed. Like other Idealists, too, Oakeshott sees these modes not as methods of understanding that are designed to deal with particular phenomena, but rather as attempts at understanding experience as a whole that do not completely succeed, so that (for example) 'Science' is not an intellectual discipline solely designed for analysing natural (as opposed to human) phenomena but rather an attempt at achieving complete coherence that fails to transcend certain presuppositions concerning causality and quantity. But he departs significantly from the other Idealists in two respects, both of which underline the importance he attaches to respecting the autonomy of the modes, rather than to proving their inadequacy. First, in contrast to virtually all the other Idealists, Oakeshott insists that the most developed modes of experience, namely 'History', 'Science' and 'Practice' are entirely independent of one another, so that conclusions reached under the auspices of one mode are completely irrelevant to the conclusions reached in another. So whilst we may, for example, decide to understand past events either purely historically or as a practical guide to the present, any attempt to combine the two conclusions will lead at best to ambiguity, and at worst to complete confusion. This position departs from that of virtually all other Idealists, and in particular from that of R. G. Collingwood, who had claimed in *Speculum Mentis* (1924), shortly before *Experience and Its Modes*, that the conclusions of each of what he considered to be the major modes of art, religion, science and history were cumulatively exposed as being inadequate by those of the succeeding ones,[17] the process ultimately culminating in the perfection of philosophy.[18] And it even differs from that of Bradley, the Idealist whom Oakeshott was closest to, since despite the fact that Bradley declines to place modes of experience on a hierarchical scale, he nevertheless argues that a complete metaphysics would demand such an ordering, hence underlining how exceptional Oakeshott insistence on the modes' mutual irrelevance is.[19] Second, much more than other Idealists, Oakeshott conceives of the developed modes of 'History', 'Science' and 'Practice' as independent of the influence of philosophizing, arguing that although philosophy can supersede the modes by pointing out the fundamental contradictions inherent in their claims to be fully coherent, it cannot be any kind of substitute for them. For instead of philosophy drawing substance from the individual modes, and hence providing the kind of knowledge that could be fruitfully applied in practice, for Oakeshott philosophy plays an almost entirely critical function, able to criticize modes for their fundamental misapprehension of the nature of experience, but not to provide any kind of knowledge that can be used instead – philosophy and the modes essentially exist, therefore, in a relationship of mutual irrelevance. And what this points to, finally, is that although Oakeshott purportedly respects the Idealists' monistic conception of experience in *Experience and Its Modes*, in fact he constantly undercuts it by stressing how self-sufficient each of the modes are, maintaining that each mode is 'free and self-contained' because 'it has put itself outside the main current of experience and made a home for itself' (Oakeshott 1933: 75). For in contrast to what Oakeshott labels 'pseudo-modes', examples of which include ethics, theology and political philosophy, and which Oakeshott believes to be easily revealed to be unstable mixtures of theory and practice by philosophical criticism, the developed modes each have a high degree of homogeneity and coherence, which can be proved ultimately inadequate, rather than intellectually incoherent, by the criticisms of philosophy.

What is really innovative, therefore, about Oakeshott's argument in *Experience and Its Modes* is not that it represents an Idealist account of experience, but rather its insistence on the value of the major modes of understanding. As such, before proceeding to examine how Oakeshott develops his account of the modes and adapts his position to pay greater attention to both political questions and the nature of tradition in his later work, we will briefly give an account of the nature of these modes. Since, however, Oakeshott fleshes out his account of the historical mode considerably in his later work whilst at the same time retaining largely the same position, we will delay examining 'History' until section three, here confining ourselves to the other modes of 'Science' and 'Practice'.

Turning first to Oakeshott's account of 'Science', therefore, in contrast to other Idealists Oakeshott goes out of his way to emphasize the degree to which this mode is a developed and sophisticated way of trying to understand the world. For although often characterized as a trenchant critic of scientific positivism, on the basis of his constant criticisms of positivist approaches to history and education, in fact, as far as 'Science' itself is concerned, Oakeshott attempts to give the mode as much coherence as possible by insisting on a highly positivist conception of scientific understanding. As one might expect, this leads him to try and eliminate the use of any metaphysical entities in formulating scientific method, since, whatever their other differences, all positivists seek, as far as possible, to discard claims about phenomena that are not subject to any kind of empirical testing. But Oakeshott in fact goes further than this, insisting that the aim of 'Science' must be to produce purely quantitative generalizations, discarding any 'common-sense' concepts whatsoever, hence showing himself to be a particularly strict kind of positivist. Key to understanding why Oakeshott adopts this position is to recognize that he models his general conception of scientific understanding on a particular view of physics, and as such insists on conceptualizing nature as an entirely mechanical entity, as 'a quantitatively conceived whole of interconnected parts such that every variation within that whole is seen to be a quantitative change' (Oakeshott 1933: 191), excluding as far as possible any purely qualitative definitions, so that scientific results can be universally agreed upon. And the insistence on this position leads Oakeshott to draw two further inferences.

First, since, as a matter of definition phenomena are viewed by the scientific mode as quantitative and mechanistic, it necessarily follows that any genuine scientific explanation – indistinguishable from description, as far as Oakeshott is concerned (Oakeshott 1933: 177 n. 1) – will be a mechanical one, taking the concepts of quantity and motion as fundamental. And despite the fact that this contradicts the way in which sciences such as geology and biology are studied in practice, Oakeshott holds firm to his contention, arguing that all this proves is that 'the present world of science is imperfectly scientific', since not all sciences have successfully followed physics in eliminating non-quantitative concepts – such as 'race' in biology, to give but one prominent example (Oakeshott 1933: 192 n. 1). Second, Oakeshott's insistence on the importance of mechanistic explanations, and his determination to eliminate as many qualitative concepts as possible leads him to espouse a particular conception of scientific method, where there are just three main stages. In the first place, the scientist must begin with certain basic concepts, labelled as 'analytic' by Oakeshott, which consist of certain fundamental mechanical generalizations. (These include, for example, the conclusion that gravity is proportional to inertia, that energy and momentum are conserved and that the extension of a body is proportional to the force acting upon it [Oakeshott 1933: 183].) Having established these, and, crucially, having established their respective relationships to one another, so that they are genuinely integrated as far as possible, the scientist can then proceed to formulate hypotheses on the basis of these initial generalizations. Such hypotheses must be designed to produce a statistical result which can contribute, ultimately, to a precise, quantitative generalized conclusion, although it should be stressed that the generalization produced will not simply be the result of induction, but will rather be a statistical average. As such, Oakeshott maintains, rather than such a generalization being one that is merely 'collective or enumerative', instead it represents a judgment about a complex whole (Oakeshott 1933: 183). Finally, having drawn up these statistical generalizations, according to Oakeshott, we may use them to try and predict future events, although since the generalizations we possess represent averages as opposed to law-like statements, these predictions will always have to be couched in terms of probability, not certainty. For because the generalization the scientist possesses is formed from the results they have gathered up until now, it cannot be applied with absolute certainty to future occurrences since they, by definition, will to a certain extent be outside its scope. What the generalizations obtained do potentially allow us to gauge, Oakeshott thinks, is how probable they are – though how well they do this will obviously be dependent on the accuracy of the original generalizations (see Oakeshott 1933: 188).

Finally, having given an exposition of what he considers correct scientific method, Oakeshott then seeks briefly to explore the implications this has for the social, as well as the natural sciences. As one might expect, since he takes the distinctions between modes as absolute, Oakeshott is adamantly opposed to any attempt to combine scientific and non-scientific approaches, as a number of social scientists at the end of the nineteenth and beginning of the twentieth century, including Max Weber, attempted to do, let alone try to make them genuinely practical disciplines. Instead, Oakeshott maintains that the social sciences, just as much as the natural ones, must either conform to the dictates of 'Science' or fail to be coherent intellectual disciplines – unless, alternatively, they succeed in qualifying as historical ones. Social sciences, in other words, must be as quantitative and value-free as natural ones according to Oakeshott, and he believes that economics and psychology can both be legitimately pursued in this manner, though he is less confident that one can do the same with anthropology. Addressing the case of the former, he believes that the objections often put forward to studying economics scientifically – in particular because the discipline deals with human behaviour, which is necessarily inexact and unpredictable as well as being immune from systematic experiment, it is resistant to such analysis – have already been largely overcome. For because economics has already established some genuinely abstract concepts – by replacing qualitative ones such as 'wealth' with authentically quantitative ones like 'price' – it is now becoming capable of formulating genuinely scientific, statistical generalizations which successfully bypass any such objections (Oakeshott 1933: 231). Equally, although psychology is much less advanced as a genuine 'science' than economics, Oakeshott sees no reason why it should not develop into one, provided that it concentrates on substituting genuinely measurable concepts – such as 'stimuli' and 'reaction' – for the present imperfectly quantitative ones – such as 'sensation' and 'attention', (Oakeshott 1933: 240) eschewing, if necessary, concepts which cannot be reformulated in this way, such as 'memory' and 'consciousness' (Oakeshott 1933: 240).[20] By contrast, Oakeshott is far less sanguine that anthropology can ever be reformulated as a genuine science – or at least one ever likely to produce interesting results. For even if one could overcome the difficulty of formulating conceptions of 'society' and 'man' sufficiently different from those of biology, psychology or economics to make establishing such a science worthwhile, Oakeshott contends, it would still be very difficult to obtain enough genuinely quantitative results about anthropological topics – such as the effects of a particular creed on different communities – to make such a science fruitful (Oakeshott 1933: 241). Far better, Oakeshott thinks, to formulate anthropology as an historical discipline.

If 'Science' represents a mode of understanding that is both highly developed and sophisticated – as we shall later see 'History' is too, as far as Oakeshott is concerned – then his view of 'Practice' in *Experience and Its Modes* is significantly different. For although like 'Science' and 'History' Oakeshott counts 'Practice' as a major mode, one of the most important ways which mankind has developed to understand the world, its most important features actually reveal it to be importantly dissimilar to the others. Like 'Science' or 'History', Oakeshott maintains that 'Practice' is largely resistant to the claims of philosophy to show it to be incoherent – so that, as with the other major modes, philosophy can only overcome practice by rejecting its fundamental postulates, not by showing it to be trivially defective. (Thus he writes, for example, that the 'world of concrete reality' can 'supersede the world of practical experience, but can never take its place' [Oakeshott 1933: 321].) But as soon as one examines the two key features of 'Practice', its difference to the other modes rapidly becomes clear.

First, Oakeshott maintains that a central facet of 'Practice' is its ubiquity, so that it is especially difficult to escape its influence, compared to that of the other modes. For by contrast with 'History', 'Science' and particularly 'Philosophy', which are severely theoretical kinds of understanding that have to be consciously undertaken, he maintains, 'Practice' is a mode that humans have to struggle hard to evade since 'our very instincts appear to concede to this world of practical ideas the presumption that here . . . lies the world of concrete reality' (Oakeshott 1933: 248). And if to some extent scientific understanding has increasingly become something of a rival to 'Practice' in modernity, Oakeshott argues, this is precisely because 'Science' has been erroneously represented as a mode that is capable of providing practical guidance. Rather than showing Science's increased ability to emancipate itself from the 'despotism of practice', a process that has been 'slow and uncertain' (Oakeshott 1933: 248), Oakeshott argues in other words, the continued attempts by what should be genuinely scientific disciplines like economics to try and justify themselves by offering practical recommendations merely highlight the difficulty of escaping the practical mode. Second, more substantively, what is striking about Oakeshott's delineation of the nature of 'Practice' is how diffuse and badly integrated the mode is by comparison with the others, essentially because the mode itself consists of an attempt at making two highly distinct worlds coherent, namely the world of 'what is here and now' and that of 'what is to come'.[21] Given the nature of the mode, by definition such an attempt must be practical rather than theoretical, but nevertheless, as an attempt to produce coherence it necessarily involves thought – it cannot simply consist of acting upon dislocated whims. This means, as far as Oakeshott is concerned, that human agents in the practical mode are constantly locked into an attempt to act in such a way as to produce 'what ought to be', to reconcile the division between 'fact' and 'value'. But such a reconciliation proves extraordinarily difficult. For as soon as an agent has remedied what is wrong in a given situation, the very fact that they are in a novel situation will affect their view of 'what ought to be', according to Oakeshott, hence leaving them with a new task. Indeed, even worse, Oakeshott argues, 'we may find that even the "ought not" of one moment is the "ought" of another' (Oakeshott 1933: 291). In such circumstances, Oakeshott maintains, the only respite we can have from this crippling division between fact and value is in religion, a phenomenon which (he believes) has nothing to do with either superstition or theology but instead represents 'practical life at its fullest', so that it 'is the consummation of all attempts to change or maintain our practical existence' (Oakeshott 1933: 294). But although such an attempt at integrating our conduct in this way can certainly help us to abate the constant pressure in practice to overcome the division between fact and value, it remains deeply difficult to do consistently – since 'in actual experience, the conduct of life as a whole . . . is not [often] . . . discharged with the same degree of . . . completeness, intensity and coherence', since 'most men . . . have neither the courage nor the energy to make [it] permanent' (Oakeshott 1933: 295). And hence the abiding impression left by Oakeshott's description of the practical mode is the deep and profound split within it between the world of 'what is' and world of 'what is to be'.

Politics, Rationalism and the Conversation of Mankind

After *Experience and Its Modes*, at first sight Oakeshott's work seems to take a completely different turn. Declining to publish another intricately written book-length study until the appearance of *On Human Conduct* in 1975, Oakeshott instead contents himself with producing various articles and essays written in a much more impressionistic and often polemical style, collecting some of the more significant in *Rationalism in Politics*, a volume that earned Oakeshott a great deal of attention. More substantively too, the nature of his work seems to change radically, because of three new developments in his writings. First, in contrast to *Experience and Its Modes*, where insofar as politics is considered at all it appears to be simply part of 'Practice', and where by implication normative political theory is dismissed (like normative ethical judgments) as a mere confusion of philosophy and practice, Oakeshott's focus becomes far more overtly political, intent on upholding individual freedom rather than the pre-eminence of the state. Second, rather than arguing that the major modes that have emerged in modernity are simply in need of some revision and clarification, Oakeshott, in some essays at least, queries whether Western intellectual development since the Enlightenment has been beneficial at all, given that it has seen a massive overemphasis on the value of technique and planning as opposed to more practical ways of thinking, with highly negative consequences in many human activities. Finally, not only does Oakeshott add another mode of understanding to his scheme, suggesting that 'Contemplation' is another *bona fide* way of understanding the world in addition to History, Science and Practice, he also changes his mind somewhat about the past philosophers that are of most interest to him, downplaying the Idealists for a newfound passion for Hobbes and Hobbesian individualism.

However, to put the case in this manner is to overstate it. For in fact, despite the unquestionably new ingredients in Oakeshott's work in this period, the essays that Oakeshott produces in the 1940s, 1950s and early 1960s also contain much that is familiar from his earlier writings – they represent a development and revision of the arguments presented in *Experience and Its Modes* as much as a total repudiation of them. Rather than representing a complete rejection of his earlier work, in other words, and its replacement by an entirely new, fully formed philosophical system, Oakeshott's essays in this period are more accurately seen as gradual and tentative attempts to explore issues that remain unresolved in *Experience and Its Modes*, especially concerning the nature of 'Practice', and the relationship between philosophy and the modes more generally – albeit that they do so in a new philosophical climate, and alongside an interest in new subjects. Furthermore, it is crucial to note that, despite its overemphasis by a number of commentators, the period in which Oakeshott criticizes the Enlightenment is actually a fairly short one, soon being replaced with a renewed, if subtly different, commitment to the achievements of modernity. Here too, in other words, despite some worries about the pervasive effects of rationalism, Oakeshott remains generally convinced of the benefits of modernity, advocating strikingly modernistic conceptions of both history and aesthetics, as well as increasingly also a particular kind of modernist individualism on a political level. To show this, and examine Oakeshott's arguments in this period more closely, we will first examine how he attempts to apply his philosophical position, as established in *Experience and Its Modes* to politics in the 1930s, following this with a discussion of how his arguments concerning both practice and tradition gradually alter in the 1940s and 1950s, although far from out of all recognition. This helps to explain Oakeshott's conversion to a particular kind of modern individualism – a position he later elaborates much more fully in *On Human Conduct*. Finally, we will also examine Oakeshott's large scale essay on 'The Voice of Poetry in the Conversation of Mankind', a piece that not only provides us with a detailed exposition of an entirely new mode, but also returns to the vexed question of the relationship of philosophy and the modes. As such it nicely exemplifies the more general point about Oakeshott's work in this period: there is both change, but also continuity.

If we turn first, therefore, to the way in which Oakeshott thinks about politics in the 1930s, we find him tentatively trying out a number of different strategies to try and analyse this aspect of human life, partly seeking to follow the arguments put forward in *Experience and Its Modes*, but also experimenting with approaches that contradict that work. Thus in his substantial essay, 'The Concept of a Philosophical Jurisprudence', he essentially puts forward an Idealist analysis of the philosophy of law and civil society, seeking to rebut the idea that such an inquiry is simply another alternative to other ways of understanding these phenomena, insisting instead on philosophy's pre-eminence. Advocating an analysis of the law that is entirely in line with the position espoused in *Experience and Its Modes*, in other words, Oakeshott rejects the possibility that any of the major ways of thinking about the law that have evolved – namely 'analytical jurisprudence', 'historical jurisprudence', 'sociological jurisprudence' and 'economic jurisprudence' – can represent serious alternatives to a genuinely philosophical understanding, since they are by definition abstract and partial, reliant upon a particular postulate that cannot be questioned without causing the approach in question to be superseded. Instead, Oakeshott maintains, a genuine philosophical analysis of the law must consist of the 'process of getting rid of, or of resolving, the presuppositions and reservations contained in whatever concepts are presented for examination' (Oakeshott 1938: 346), and, as such, logically implies the overcoming of all abstract modes by a form of understanding that is as completely coherent and concrete as possible. In line with his earlier work, therefore, Oakeshott rules out the idea that a genuine philosophical analysis of the law can consist of applying a special kind of preconceived knowledge – rather, according to him, it implies the transformation of legal concepts that are already in existence out of all recognition. And because of this, just as in *Experience and Its Modes*, Oakeshott argues that this leaves no room for the philosophy of law to be a normative exercise – since the latter pursuit is by definition a practical and not a philosophical inquiry.

By contrast, in other works written in the 1930s, particularly later in the decade, Oakeshott departs from the position put forward in *Experience and Its Modes*, to some extent focusing more on practical political questions, rather than determining the limits of ethics and political philosophy, and even raising the possibility of there being a closer, more reciprocal relationship between theory and practice than envisaged in his earlier work. Thus despite remaining aloof from practical politics for much of the 1930s, notoriously instead focusing some of his energies on writing a teasingly entitled book on horse-racing (Oakeshott and Griffith 1936), as we saw in chapter one, even Oakeshott felt impelled by the events of Munich in 1938 (encouraged by the intervention of his friend Ernest Barker) to compile an anthology considering the nature of the most important 'social and political doctrines of contemporary Europe', these being representative democracy, Catholicism, communism, Fascism and National Socialism. Even here, Oakeshott is anxious to downplay the idea that the value of any particular kind of political practice can be measured by the extent to which it can be theoretically articulated, but he does at least concede that 'when a [political] regime *chooses* to rationalize its practice . . . the coherence of such a statement becomes a matter or importance; and if it can be convicted of intellectual confusion, that is not a fault that can be brushed aside as insignificant' (Oakeshott 1939: xv – emphasis mine). In particular, despite the studied neutrality with which he puts forward his analysis, Oakeshott maintains that communism, Fascism and National Socialism all suffer by comparison with the other two, in ways that subsequently become significant in his later work, namely that they lack a proper appreciation of the importance of tradition, and accede to the handing over to a group of self-appointed leaders the planning of the entire life of a society. (By contrast, 'to the Liberal and Catholic mind alike the notion that men can authoritatively plan and impose a way of life upon a society appears to be a piece of pretentious ignorance' [Oakeshott 1939: xxii n.1].) And more theoretically, in the essay 'The Claims of Politics', written soon after in 1939, although Oakeshott writes contemptuously of the nature of politics itself, arguing that it 'is neither the only adequate expression, nor the overwhelmingly most important expression of a sensibility for the communal interests of a society' (Oakeshott 1993b: 94), and that it is an activity which necessarily requires 'a mind fixed and callous to all subtle distinctions' (Oakeshott 1993b: 93), he nevertheless also here stresses the importance of some kind of theoretical articulation in safeguarding the health of society, again in defiance of the absolute separation of theory and practice insisted upon in *Experience and Its Modes*. Rather than this theoretical articulation being a political one, however, Oakeshott argues that it will be the work of the artist – or possibly the philosopher – so that through their work, 'a society [potentially] becomes conscious and critical of itself' (Oakeshott 1993b: 95), hence protecting it from a 'corruption of its consciousness' (Oakeshott 1993b: 95) through the illumination and analysis of its crucial values and premises. And if in maintaining this claim Oakeshott was partly picking up themes he had explored much earlier in his career, before the austere separation of theory and practice propagated in *Experience and Its Modes* – most notably in an 'Essay on the Relations of Philosophy, Poetry and Reality' – more immediately he may well have been responding to a similar argument made by Collingwood in his recently published *Principles of Art*, a work Oakeshott had recently favourably reviewed (Oakeshott 1937/8: 487). Indeed, the very phrase 'the corruption of consciousness' is Collingwood's.[22]

These essays from the 1930s can certainly help us to gain a fuller picture of Oakeshott's intellectual development after the publication of *Experience and Its Modes*. However, despite this, and to some extent being interesting in themselves, ultimately they remain tentative pieces which at best hint at Oakeshott's later development, and at worst merely represent cul-de-sacs – not least for Oakeshott himself. (It is surely significant, for example, that, despite being a substantial piece of work, the 'Concept of a Philosophical Jurisprudence' is not collected by Oakeshott in *Rationalism in Politics and Other Essays*, unlike at least one other piece from the 1930s.) By contrast, in the aftermath of the Second World War, Oakeshott began to produce a much more distinctive set of essays, often published in the *Cambridge Journal*, which, although still less closely argued than *Experience and Its Modes*, nevertheless clearly represented the emergence of a more definite position, concentrated in particular on a suspicion of rationalistic planning and a concomitant insistence on the importance of tradition and knowledge learned in practice. This was obviously partly inspired by the experiences of the Second World War, and a resultant suspicion of anything that smacked of Nazism or communism – though even here, as we have seen, Oakeshott expressed objections along these lines before the Second World War. But the essays also, on another level, represented a desire on Oakeshott's part to refine the nature of the 'practical' mode, to resolve some of the unsatisfactory aspects of the position put forward in *Experience and Its Modes*, by re-examining the way in which human agents act in practice more closely, and rejecting some of the more abstract analysis put forward in the earlier work, which in some respects was more focused on establishing the contradictory nature of 'Practice' than on working out exactly what motivates human action. In doing so, Oakeshott took time to work out his final position so that, although by far the most famous essay from this period – and arguably of his whole career – the article 'Rationalism in Politics' (1947) represents the beginning rather than the end of this process. As such, we also need to pay close attention to Oakeshott's other essays from this period to see the way his thought developed. Before that, however, it is unquestionably 'Rationalism in Politics' that we must next examine.

In this essay, Oakeshott is at his most radical and polemical. For not merely is his aim to criticize the practical effects of the Attlee government's penchant for planning, or even, more widely, to take issue with the commonly held view in the 1940s that the experiences of the Second World War had proved the superiority of collectivism in peacetime as well as in wartime – though these were logical implications of his view – but rather to make a more far-reaching point. Instead what he seeks to do is to attack what he sees as the faulty epistemological position underlying the popularity of planning, which mistakenly claims that all knowledge can be reduced to consciously formulated propositions that can be unproblematically applied in practice. This is the position Oakeshott labels 'rationalism', and he argues that it is a direct consequence of the Enlightenment's suspicion of anything that cannot be directly justified by reason, so that the rationalist is sceptical of 'authority, of prejudice, of the merely traditional customary or habitual' (Oakeshott 1991: 6) – although equally optimistic that all problems can be solved with the help of a mind that is 'well-trained rather than . . . [well] educated' (Oakeshott 1991: 7). Essentially, therefore, what the rationalist denies is the possibility that there is a form of knowledge that cannot be precisely formulated, that resists reduction to 'rules, principles, directions [and] maxims', which cannot be 'learned from a book . . . repeated by rote, and applied mechanically', and instead 'exists only in use, is not reflective' and 'can neither be taught nor learned, but only imparted and acquired' (Oakeshott 1991: 12). Oakeshott calls this 'practical knowledge' – in contrast to the other kind which he labels 'technical knowledge' – and, in sharp contrast to the rationalist, he insists that practical knowledge is always necessary for the successful performance of any kind of human activity; to claim otherwise is to be seriously mistaken. Such knowledge, Oakeshott argues, consists in such things as the artistry a pianist gains at the same time as learning technique, the insight into positions a chess-player gains as well as knowledge of the moves and the judgment that a scientist acquires to show when his technique is leading him astray (Oakeshott 1991: 15); and he argues that it is always very closely linked to the technical knowledge. It is not the case, for example, that one can distinguish between practical and technical knowledge by claiming the distinction corresponds to one between 'means' and 'ends', or even that the difference is that technical knowledge tells us 'what' to do, while practical knowledge tells us 'how' to do it. For 'even in the what . . . there lies already this dualism of technique and practice', Oakeshott maintains, giving the illustration of a doctor's diagnosis as an example.[23] In short, therefore, although in 'Rationalism in Politics' Oakeshott maintains that technical and practical knowledge are completely discrete, he also argues that they are utterly inseparable.

As stated, part of Oakeshott's purpose in 'Rationalism in Politics' is to trace back the three essential tenets of modern rationalism – namely that knowledge must be discovered through a precisely formulated set of directions, that can be applied purely mechanically and can be used universally – to its Enlightenment founders, namely Bacon and Descartes.

And if Oakeshott blames Bacon more than Descartes for the modern rationalist's overconfidence, since he maintains Descartes had a more sceptical streak to his thought, he nevertheless excuses both to some extent, arguing that it was their followers (rather than the thinkers themselves) who insisted upon the indispensability of rationalist dogma, dismissing the value of practical knowledge on this basis.[24] Equally, however, in 'Rationalism in Politics', and throughout his essays of the 1940s and 1950s, Oakeshott is at least as keen to illustrate the negative consequences of rationalism on politics in particular, partly because this was simply the discipline he had become most interested in, but also because he believed that politics (surprisingly) was the area of society that had become most infected with rationalist thinking. So instead of being, as one might have expected, the aspect of modern society that presented some resistance to rationalism, Oakeshott argues, in fact so much has trust in tradition and 'the politics of repair' given way to a reliance on consciously formulated political ideologies and 'the politics of destruction and creation' (Oakeshott 1991: 26), that even supposed opponents of rationalism in politics (such as Hayek) actually couch their opposition in rationalist terms. No doubt 'a plan to resist all planning may be better than its opposite', Oakeshott dismissively concedes, but 'it belongs to the same style of politics' (Oakeshott 1991: 26).

What does Oakeshott hold responsible for the growth of rationalism in politics, and how does he think this influence should be countered? In 'Rationalism in Politics' itself, and in 'The Tower of Babel', an essay written shortly after, Oakeshott's answers to these questions are relatively compressed and vague. To explain the rise of rationalism, he cites the involvement of more inexperienced people in politics over the last four centuries, arguing that the advent of new kinds of rulers, followed by a new ruling class and finally by a new political society, has led to an unprecedented demand for 'cribs' – in other words for rationalistically formulated principles that can stand as some kind of substitute for a lack of proper knowledge of political tradition, for a lack of political education. For each case, Oakeshott provides what he considers representative examples, citing Machiavelli's writings on politics as an example of a crib for a new ruler, Locke's *Second Treatise of Civil Government* and the work of Marx and Engels as examples of cribs for politically inexperienced ruling classes; and the nature of American politics (both before and after the founding of the constitution) as emblematic of a society in which only rationalistic principles (rather than political tradition) are valued (Oakeshott 1991: 28–33). But in politics as in every other kind of human activity, Oakeshott argues, such consciously formulated political ideologies can be no substitute for genuine practical knowledge, and the net effect of relying on such ideologies is a constant lurching from crisis to perceived crisis, as the rationalist attempt to 'solve' each political 'problem' by the mechanical application of political 'principles'. Instead, according to Oakeshott, it is essential that we use the inherited wisdom of our political tradition, not ignoring the contribution that can be made by technical knowledge – since political principles have an important role to play – but giving tradition its proper (pre-eminent) place in determining how we should act politically. More particularly, Oakeshott argues in 'The Tower of Babel', what the self-conscious use of moral rules – and even more of moral ideals – lacks is the flexibility that is inherent in a proper use of our moral and political tradition. For relying on one's tradition, he argues, is not to submit to a changeless condition where the only hope of relief comes from the imposition from outside of a formulated moral ideal (Oakeshott 1991: 471–2); rather Oakeshott maintains: 'there is a freedom and inventiveness at the heart of every traditional way of life, and deviation may be an expression of that freedom, springing from a sensitiveness to the tradition itself and remaining faithful to the traditional form' (Oakeshott 1991: 472). So whilst there is a place for the technical knowledge of moral rules and political ideology, Oakeshott submits, their traditional counterparts must take priority.

This then is how Oakeshott conceptualizes tradition and criticizes rationalism in the late 1940s, and what rapidly becomes clear is that his position, whilst both stimulating and suggestive, leaves several important questions about the conceptualization of tradition and practical knowledge unanswered. To some extent, we can understand what he is saying better simply by referring to his earlier work as put forward in *Experience and Its Modes,* and notably to his contention that because anything less than a completely self-conscious and complete conceptualization of experience is bound to lead to abstraction, any other kinds of reflection to some extent distort and change the original practical experience. Any kind of self-conscious reflections on our practical experiences, in other words – however interesting and worthwhile the results – can never be a complete substitute for them, and is the folly of the rationalist to think that they can be. (As Oakeshott puts it in 'Rationalism in Politics': 'the Rationalist is always in the unfortunate position of not being able to touch anything without transforming it into an abstraction; he can never get a square meal of experience' [Oakeshott 1991: 31 n. 30].) However, although this helps us clarify Oakeshott's position somewhat, it still leaves us with two important questions unanswered, questions which lead Oakeshott to alter and refine his position during the course of the 1950s. First, although Oakeshott is clear in 'Rationalism in Politics' that practical knowledge alone is always insufficient for the successful performance of any human activity, so that some form of technical knowledge is also essential – in this consciously following the position of Michael Polanyi, as put forward in *Science, Faith and Society* (1946) and elsewhere (see Polayni 1958, passim) – this leaves the problem of how the two forms of knowledge are related unexplained. In particular it leaves unanswered the question of how technical knowledge concerning a particular activity was acquired in the first place, if it is something that is supposed to be entirely separate from one's practical ability in the same area.[25] This was a problem that had in a sense been solved by the time Oakeshott was writing the essays 'Rational Conduct' (1950) and 'Political Education' (1951) – since by this point he had altered his position to claim that technical knowledge is necessarily an abstraction, something that is always derived from practical knowledge, without an independent existence of its own. This in turn was the result of Oakeshott significantly changing the way in which he conceived of human agents performing actions and practices in general, so that in these essays, and throughout his later work as a whole, he comes to maintain that there is no such thing as rationality outside of the ability to perform practices. What Oakeshott was latterly arguing, in other words, probably under the influence of Gilbert Ryle (compare Ryle 1949: 26–60), was that any account of action which posited an agent deciding upon the nature of the end they are pursuing in advance of choosing a practice was fundamentally mistaken; rather, he maintains, an agent's actions are always performed relative to a particular tradition of behaviour, so that (for example) 'a cook is not a man who first has vision of a pie and then tries to make it; he is a man skilled in cookery, and both his projects and his achievements spring from that skill' (Oakeshott 1991: 111).[26] Oakeshott's position here is extremely radical – even compared to Ryle and Wittgenstein, who make similar arguments in favour of the primacy of practical reasoning – since he maintains that the rationality associated with each practical ability is entirely discrete and non-transferable. This is probably not ultimately very convincing, since it seems likely that our practical abilities are more closely linked than this – so that, for example, an ability to practice law might well help us to understand how to perform in political life better. But it is at least more internally coherent than the position Oakeshott puts forward in 'Rationalism in Politics', giving a better explanation of how technical and practical knowledge are related.

The second problem with the way in which Oakeshott conceptualizes tradition in 'Rationalism in Politics', is that he seems to be making a descriptive ontological claim about it, rather than putting forward a normative argument. Instead of establishing that modern politics suffers from being insufficiently sensitive towards the importance of tradition, it would seem that the net effect of Oakeshott's argument in this essay is simply to point out that political actors are necessarily always conditioned by the tradition within which they are performed – so that it is literally impossible to engage in political activity without recourse to some kind of traditional knowledge. But if this is the case, Oakeshott is left with no means of objecting, normatively, to the way that society has developed – if all is traditional, in other words, nothing can be reprehensible. So if a country develops a tradition that favours extensive government intervention, or a lack of respect for authority, or even discrimination against certain racial groups, there seems to be no way of objecting to such traditions, according to this position.

To deal with this problem, Oakeshott puts forward a number of potential solutions, gradually adapting his position over the course of the 1950s and 1960s. First, he simply tries to maintain that, since tradition is not conceived of as monolithic, but rather as inevitably diverse, it always has sufficient resources to repair itself if it runs into trouble. Because a wide variety of courses of action will be sanctioned by tradition at any given point in time, in other words, it does not follow that we must automatically follow any one particular norm; this is to mistake the nature of the concept. Rather, through debate and discussion – through 'conversation', to use one of Oakeshott's favoured terms – political actors will decide which of the many courses of action on offer they will choose to take. So if a political system has taken a wrong turn, therefore, there is no reason to suppose that it cannot remedy itself, provided its tradition is sufficiently rich in conceptual resources to allow this to happen.

However, if this argument corrected the impression that Oakeshott was simply advocating the blind following of the latest norms provided by tradition, then it provided little help in offering a genuinely normative alternative to bad political practices. If racism – just to take one example – is a firm component of a political tradition, even if only a subsidiary one, then there is no particular reason why political discussion and debate will lead to its elimination. In view of this, Oakeshott's next attempted solution was to flirt with the possibility that the Western tradition as a whole had malfunctioned at some point with the introduction of false rationalist tenets, sometimes suggesting that this had occurred during the Enlightenment (in 'Rationalism in Politics') and sometimes even earlier during the first five centuries after the introduction of Christianity (in 'The Tower of Babel'). In common with a number of twentieth-century critics of modernity, such as Eric Voegelin, Leo Strauss and (more ambiguously) Hannah Arendt, in such places Oakeshott seemed to be hinting that we can object to undesirable contemporary political developments by advocating a return to a point earlier in the tradition before it became corrupted, whether this be before the Enlightenment or even earlier. Such an argument certainly provided Oakeshott with a genuine normative platform to object to rationalism in modern political life, but only at the cost of turning him into an advocate of strident anti-modernism. This was something that (as we have seen) he had been resistant to in his earlier work, being a strong advocate of pluralism, at least at the epistemological level – unlike the anti-modernists like Strauss. For Strauss, modern pluralism was a consequence of mankind not being in harmony with natural law, so that it falsely posited a diversity of equally good ways to understand the world in contrast to the one true one. This was an option, therefore, that Oakeshott never showed much sign of embracing with enthusiasm – despite some commentators' valiant attempts to prove the contrary.[27]

In view of these difficulties, from the middle of the 1950s at the latest, Oakeshott began to reformulate his position. Instead of conceptualizing 'tradition' purely philosophically as either something that is simply regulative, that exists as an inescapable background condition whenever agents act or alternatively as something monolithic, as a single accumulated set of experiences that is capable of falling into error *in toto*, Oakeshott shifts to analysing tradition in more genuinely historical terms. Thus in such works as 'The Masses in Representative Democracy' (1957), the Harvard lectures *Morality and Politics in Modern Europe* (1958), and ultimately the third essay in *On Human Conduct*, Oakeshott seeks to identify the most important trend in the Western European tradition, arguing that this consists of the gradual emergence of individualism in theory and practice from the twelfth and thirteenth centuries onwards, and the concomitant loosening of the communal ties and self-identifications of the medieval period (Oakeshott 1991: 365–6).Whilst far from being universally welcomed, Oakeshott concedes, since many resented (or at least lamented) the loss of warm communal relationships enjoyed in such medieval institutions as corporations, churches and village communities, and hence attempted to recreate such relationships in a modern context by urging love of 'the community', to be fostered by a morality of the 'common good', the gradual rise of modern individualism nevertheless presented Western European men and women with unprecedented opportunities for self-development and self-expression. For due to the advent of privacy above all, Oakeshott maintains, modern individuals were given both an opportunity and a stimulus to explore their own personal inclinations, something that they soon began to value as 'the main ingredient of "happiness"', and which were celebrated in a variety of highly sophisticated ways by theorists as diverse as Montaigne, Hobbes, Spinoza and (above all) Kant (Oakeshott 1991: 367). Almost inevitably, Oakeshott argues, this led to a much greater diversity of individual experience than in the medieval periods, something that gives him every reason to continue to object to the attempt to reduce the plurality of moral and political experiences to self-conscious moral and political rules and ideals. But if in his earlier post-war essays this was for an epistemological reason – that any attempt to reduce traditional knowledge to self-conscious maxims was bound to end in at least partial failure – the reason was now fundamentally a moral and historical one, namely, that such an attempt would fail to respect the diversity of individual experience as it existed in modernity in Western Europe. So whilst there was considerable continuity to Oakeshott's insistence in the post-war period that trying to reduce moral and political experience to moral ideals and political ideologies was bound to lead to abstraction, the reason for this had shifted considerably by the middle of the 1950s.

Since Oakeshott comes to the view in the mid-1950s that modern pluralist individualism is not merely an important development in the Western European tradition, but also an achievement that it is vital to celebrate and encourage, it is hardly surprising that he devotes considerable time and effort in the remainder of his career to identifying the system of government that is necessary to sustain such individualism. In particular, in the essays dating from the 1940s and 1950s, such as in 'On Being Conservative', Oakeshott stresses the necessity of avoiding government that is designed to be 'a perpetual take-over bid for the purchase of the resources of human energy in order to concentrate them in a single direction' (Oakeshott 1991: 426) that seeks to unite individuals artificially around a single, pre-determined end, arguing instead that it is the business of government to respect the diversity of individual practices and desires in society, so that 'every subject . . . [is] secured of the right to pursue his chosen directions of activity as little hindered as might be by his fellows or by the exactions of government itself, and as little distracted by communal pressures' (Oakeshott 1991: 369). To do this, Oakeshott stresses, requires a government that is *sovereign* – in other words one powerful enough to be able to overcome 'the communal pressures of family and guild, of church and local community' (Oakeshott 1991: 368), and to enforce its laws successfully on the subjects that it is governing. But it must also be a government, he emphasizes, that operates according to the 'rule of law', whereby individuals are all equally subject to the same known laws, whatever their class or status, rather than being subjected to unexpected or capricious commands, or laws that have been illegitimately passed. Beyond these important but unelaborated points, however, Oakeshott provides little further detail about how one should organize the state to respect modern individualism, and it is only with the publication of *On Human Conduct* (1975) and 'The Rule of Law' (1983) that we are really given a truly detailed account of Oakeshott's political theory.

Before turning to these works, however, we need briefly to examine Oakeshott's other celebrated essay from this period, 'The Voice of Poetry in the Conversation of Mankind' (1959). Notable for being far more explicit about his epistemological pluralism than *Experience and Its Modes*, in this essay Oakeshott removes any possibility that philosophy can supersede individual modes of experience – to the extent, in fact, that he at one point labels philosophy a 'parasitic' activity which 'springs from the conversation' between modes 'but . . . makes no specific contribution to it' (Oakeshott 1991: 491). But it is also important because it marks another break with his earlier work in positing an entirely new mode – namely 'Poetry' or 'Contemplation' – to add to 'History', 'Science' and 'Practice'. In his previous work concerning artistic contemplation, Oakeshott had either identified this activity with a search for ultimate reality (in 'An Essay on the Relations of Philosophy, Poetry, and Reality') or as something that was in various ways thoroughly practical (notably in *Experience and Its Modes* and in 'The Claims of Politics'), but here reacts strongly against such views, arguing for the complete autonomy of the new 'poetic' mode. (It is true that in identifying artistic activity as 'practical' in his earlier work Oakeshott tended to mean that it was capable of heightening our perception of practical reality in some way, rather than that it would serve an overtly utilitarian purpose, but there is nevertheless no doubting the importance of the shift.) Instead, in 'The Voice of Poetry', Oakeshott argues that 'poetic' activity consists of the simple contemplation of images with a view to 'delight' in them, ruling out any possibility that this activity may have any practical benefits whatsoever, however defined. In particular, Oakeshott disputes the contention that such a contemplative experience can assist us to improve our moral sensibility by helping us to see truths concerning human character, arguing that we cannot approve or disapprove of the conduct of (for example) Othello or Daisy Miller since 'they are not people . . . who have ever inhabited the practical world of desire and enterprise, and consequently their "conduct" cannot be either "right" or "wrong" nor their dispositions "good" or "bad"' (Oakeshott 1991: 520). Furthermore, he argues, it is completely false to think we can learn something about an artist from what they are trying to express through their artwork, explicitly disputing the idea that the artist must have experienced the emotion or experience being conveyed through their artwork – poetry, in other words, is not 'the spontaneous overflow of powerful feelings' as Wordsworth and Shelley for example claim (Oakeshott 1991: 524 n. 21). And if neither of these arguments remotely convinces, since there is no reason why the fictional nature of imagined characters should prevent us from judging their experiences, and hence relating it to our own conduct, nor any particular reason why learning about an emotion should be such a personal experience that we can only learn about it from someone who has had the emotion themselves or evokes it in us, 'The Voice of Poetry' nevertheless highlights two of Oakeshott's most fundamental convictions once again. First, Oakeshott regards it as axiomatic that major modes of understanding must be entirely distinct from one another – so that, in this case, he is intent above all on keeping 'Poetry' separate from the practical mode at all costs. And, second, once again, just as with 'Science' in *Experience and Its Modes*, Oakeshott remains intent on putting forward as modernist a conception of his modes as possible – so that 'Poetry' epitomizes the modernist attitude of 'art for art's sake', in this case almost to the point of total absurdity. Despite many claims to the contrary, therefore, even in the 1940s and 1950s Oakeshott's commitment to modernity was not in doubt.

Oakeshott's Late Work: *On Human Conduct* and *On History*

After publishing *Rationalism in Politics and Other Essays* in 1962, Oakeshott took a considerable time to address the questions left unanswered by his middle-period work regarding the nature of the state, and in particular how it should be arranged to respect and encourage modern individualism. Indeed it is clear from Oakeshott's correspondence that the work he eventually produced to deal with this problem in 1975, namely *On Human Conduct*, was the result of a considerable struggle, as Oakeshott agonized over how to make his position unambiguously clear, eventually choosing to do so with the help of a new (partly Latin-derived) vocabulary. In substance the work consisted of three interconnected and densely argued essays. These examined (respectively) how Oakeshott believed 'human conduct' should be theorized about, the sort of state appropriate for modern individuals – dubbed 'the civil condition'[28] – and the nature of the modern European state in practice, which Oakeshott argued was best analysed as the combination of (or at least struggle between) two opposing conceptions, namely a purposive 'teleocratic' one, and a goalless framework that respected individual differences. Supposedly, the work was an entirely philosophical one, which seeks to analyse the nature of human conduct from a purely objective standpoint, drawing conclusions from this analysis about the kinds of state that most suit it, buttressed by an historical analysis of the way in which those kinds of state have developed in Western Europe. But despite the determination of some of Oakeshott's interpreters to take this argument at face value, it is clear that Oakeshott's analysis is based upon the particular reading of Western European history that was mentioned earlier – namely one which diagnoses individualism as the most important development in modernity, and indeed goes further in upholding it as the most important modern achievement. So although in what follows we will concentrate on examining the first two essays of *On Human Conduct*, since these are the ones that put forward Oakeshott's mature political theory, it can hardly be stressed strongly enough that these essays are dependent on the third one – namely Oakeshott's reading of Western European political history. Without appreciating this, it is impossible to see what Oakeshott is really doing.

On the theoretical understanding of *On Human Conduct*

Turning to the first essay of *On Human Conduct*, then, Oakeshott begins his analysis of how we should theorize about modern individualism with a restatement of how we should philosophize in general, in many ways recapitulating the arguments he put forward in *Experience and Its Modes*. As in the earlier work, Oakeshott denies that the process of understanding can ever begin with us simply confronting something entirely unknown; rather, what we seek to understand is always to some extent understood already – 'we inexorably inhabit a world of intelligibles' (Oakeshott 1975: 1).[29] Also as before, Oakeshott stresses that unless we are content to remain on a fairly basic level of understanding, which consists of more or less immediate identifications or recognitions, then we need to invoke the help of 'ideal characters' which allow us to explore the nature of the phenomena – or 'goings-on' – we are examining. Such 'ideal characters' may initially be fairly basic ones – such as identifying a dance as a 'fandango' – but if we keep questioning the presuppositions that make such identifications possible, then inevitably we find ourselves using much more complex ones similar to the 'modes' of Oakeshott earlier work, so that (for example) instead of simply taking the concept of 'time' as uncontested, we begin a scientific inquiry into the very concept of time itself (Oakeshott 1975: 9). And if by the time of *On Human Conduct* Oakeshott has entirely dropped the idea that philosophizing should be defined as the search for absolute coherence, he nevertheless still persists in seeing it as the unconditional questioning of presuppositions, of 'postulates', so that (for example) philosophizing about practical activities provides us with information about their presuppositions, rather than about the activities themselves. So the conclusions of philosophy remain completely inapplicable in practice.[30] It is true that there are two significant changes in Oakeshott's position in *On Human Conduct* as compared to *Experience and Its Modes*. In the first place, Oakeshott significantly changes the way in which he conceptualizes 'Practice', making it clear that it exists on a lower level of abstraction than the other modes of 'History', 'Science' and 'Poetry', distinguishing 'doing' and 'theorizing', with the unconditional theorizing of 'Philosophy' at a higher level still.[31] Secondly, Oakeshott revises the way he conceptualizes distinctions between modes, making them dependent on a prior distinction between different 'orders' of inquiry, namely between those that understand 'goings-on' as being 'exhibitions of intelligence' and those that explain them as being the result of unintelligent 'processes'. Thus disciplines such as ethics, jurisprudence and aesthetics are to be regarded as examples of the former, according to Oakeshott, whilst physics, chemistry and psychology are to be identified as examples of the latter (Oakeshott 1975: 12–15). But just as in *Experience and Its Modes*, Oakeshott continues to insist that this distinction is not an ontological one – ostensibly at least the distinction refers to different kinds of explanation, and not to any intrinsic difference in the 'goings-on' being considered. And more widely, despite the differences, there is a considerable similarity in the way philosophizing is conceptualized in the two works considered.

Having restated how to define philosophizing itself, Oakeshott then proceeds to examine how to theorize about human actions, considering in particular how to conceptualize them as 'human conduct'. First, in accordance with his new distinction between 'intelligent' and 'unintelligent' kinds of human activity, he identifies 'human conduct' as the former, though he maintains – ostensibly at least – that explaining human behaviour in terms of natural processes is equally valid. (By contrast, combining the two orders of inquiry Oakeshott regards as completely illegitimate, so that, for example, any attempt by psychologists or sociologists to reduce human behaviour that is understood to be the result of intelligent conduct to mental processes or sociological laws is to attempt an entirely confused analysis [Oakeshott 1975: 21–2].[32]) 'Intelligent' behaviour, Oakeshott maintains here, consists of any actions that are the result of 'reflective consciousness', an attribute that does not imply any particular level of self-consciousness, but simply that actions must be 'learned' responses in the widest sense of the word.[33] This in turn implies, Oakeshott argues, in many ways following an Aristotelian approach to human action, that producing a 'learned' response requires at least a minimal ability to understand one's situation and formulate coherent responses to it, arguing further that the uncertain nature of 'doing' means that the right course of action cannot be *demonstrated* deductively from certain premises, but only *deliberated* about.[34] This uncertainty, Oakeshott maintains, is largely caused by the fact that the ends agents aim at in human conduct almost always involve other agents, so that although any action begins with a particular individual's understanding of a situation, and a decision to aim at an intended outcome, such a decision is dependent on the perceived and actual responses of others. And precisely for this reason – namely that every situation in human conduct is an 'understood' one – an individual's diagnosis of a particular predicament can never be immune from the judgments of others: to quote Oakeshott himself: 'the attribution of independence in virtue of an agent's situation being what he understands it to be does not release his understanding from judgement in which it may be pronounced a misunderstanding' (Oakeshott 1975: 38).[35]

Having argued that the essence of 'human conduct' is a relationship based upon learned responses, in which the attempts of agents to achieve their ends are almost always rendered uncertain by being dependent on the responses of other agents, Oakeshott then goes on to specify the nature of human conduct more fully. In particular, he proceeds to argue that one cannot simply analyse human conduct as a set of 'ad hoc terminable encounters', in which individuals seek particular, discrete satisfactions, since this is to ignore the vital role played by 'practices'. These consist of the conventions, customs, principles and rules that affect the ways in which agents seek satisfactions and perform actions in conduct, though they cannot themselves be specifically performed – rather, they act as 'adverbial qualifiers' which 'prescribe conditions for, but does not determine, the substantive choices and performances of agents' (Oakeshott 1975: 55).[36] Such 'practices' cannot consist of relationships which are based upon force,[37] according to Oakeshott, or where agents are merely joined in the simple pursuit of a common satisfaction, since in neither instance is the freedom of agency intrinsic to human conduct being properly respected, but aside from this his definition of what 'practices' can consist of is extremely wide. Thus they can consist of something as limited as a protocol, on the one hand, or of something that can compose an entire way of life – such as stoicism or chivalry – on the other. Moreover, they can overlap, 'compose hierarchies', or join together, as far as Oakeshott is concerned, and may become as definite and firm as the workings of an institution, or else remain relatively plastic (Oakeshott 1975: 56). And they may either emerge gradually as the unintended by-products of performances or, much more unusually, be expressly designed (Oakeshott 1975: 58). Essentially what Oakeshott is doing here is to specify more exactly what he meant by 'tradition' in his middle-period essays, substituting the term 'practices' instead, so as to emphasize both the plurality inherent in his concept of 'tradition', and also the mutability – since the practices that make up a single 'tradition' evolve with each and every performance they qualify (Oakeshott 1976: 364).

Although Oakeshott does not distinguish very much between different kinds of 'practice' in *On Human Conduct*, there is one key distinction he does make between them, namely between what he calls 'prudential' and 'moral' practices. The former are defined straightforwardly as those that come into existence specifically to facilitate certain desired outcomes – so that they include the rules for making pastry, an office routine or that a train service runs strictly to timetable – but, Oakeshott stresses, not all practices take this form. In addition, he maintains, borrowing (but also modifying) a distinction made famous by Aristotle, there are also 'moral' practices that are not designed to 'produce' anything, but are instead 'concerned with good and bad conduct'. As is the case with all practices, these do not prescribe particular courses of actions, but rather 'adverbially qualify' the actions that agents perform, so that acting morally does not consist of the self-conscious application of moral rules to improve our behaviour, but rather simply using the ethical experience inherent in the tradition one is born into, and which can only be learned in practice, through interaction with others. Just as in *Rationalism in Politics,* Oakeshott is insistent that moral rules and ideals will necessarily be abstractions, insufficient to help us act morally in practice, and he underlines this point in *On Human Conduct* by stressing how similar acting morally is to speaking a vernacular language. For in the same way we learn to converse successfully with other speakers through the experience of interacting with other speakers, Oakeshott argues, rather than through the self-conscious application of grammatical and syntactical rules, so equally we learn to act morally through the experience we gain in practice, not through guides to moral behaviour. Thus as Oakeshott himself pithily puts it: 'moral conduct is not solving problems; it is agents continuously and colloquially related to one another in the idiom of a familiar language of moral converse' (Oakeshott 1975: 64).

In many ways therefore, Oakeshott's approach to morality closely resembles that of Aristotle in the *Nicomachean Ethics*. Like Aristotle, he argues that because the way an agent behaves morally necessarily involves responding to other individuals intelligently, it therefore cannot be explained either by simply referring to their anterior dispositions or analysed in terms of them deploying the same kind of skill (*techne*) that can help produce objects. For since other agents, unlike objects, are necessarily unpredictable, both Aristotle and Oakeshott maintain that utilizing the kind of mechanical skill that enables us (for example) to make tables or play the flute is not enough to allow us to act morally, since such skills essentially consist of being able to repeat the same thing over and over again successfully, rather than to respond intelligently to new situations. As such, such *technai* always remain external to an agent, and do not fundamentally affect his or her character. Instead, to act morally, both Aristotle and Oakeshott maintain, agents have to employ an entirely different ability to interact with other agents, namely what Aristotle calls *phronesis* or 'practical wisdom'. This enables agents to understand others' actions and characters and hence act appropriately in a given situation, helping to apply universal principles to individual concrete situations and to help determine both means and ends for an agent's conduct.[38] Indeed, such is its practical orientation, that it might be more accurate to say that *phronesis* helps to *transcend* such dichotomies, giving agents the ability to respond quasi-instinctively to each particular situation.[39] As such, both argue, such an ability necessarily implies using an agent's inherited experience and understanding of others in order to enable them to accomplish this, so that in contrast to *technai*, which always remains external to an agent and do not fundamentally affect his or her character, the application of *phronesis* not only reveals the nature of their character, but will also inevitably alter it, to a greater or lesser extent.

However, despite these similarities, there are also several significant differences in the way that Oakeshott and Aristotle conceptualize morality, and these are important in showing that Oakeshott's conception of 'human conduct' is reliant on a particular view of human agency – namely the highly individualist and pluralist one sketched earlier – rather than being a purely neutral philosophical analysis. First, most fundamentally, despite the many similarities of his position with Aristotle's regarding the nature of human action, Oakeshott starkly disagrees with the latter over the possibility of there being a generally agreed definition of happiness, taking it as incontrovertible that no such definition can exist, at least in modernity. As he puts it himself, using his favourite linguistic metaphor, the plurality of moral languages in the world 'cannot be resolved by being understood as . . . regrettable divergencies from a fancied perfect and universal language of moral intercourse' (Oakeshott 1975: 80), so that the idea of pursuing an objective 'human excellence' simply does not make sense. So although agents' actions and satisfactions are certainly not immune from the *understanding* of others, Oakeshott argues, in other words, nevertheless they are, potentially at least, utterly incommensurable with one another. And this has two important further implications. In the first place, it means that although *phronesis* is a vital skill for agents to possess, since it enables them to act appropriately, in accordance with the conventions of their tradition, it cannot, according to Oakeshott, offer any guide as to how to act *objectively* well, in accordance with an objective good, as it does for Aristotle, since such a thing does not exist.[40] And secondly, it also implies that there will be potentially, of necessity, an irresolvable diversity of human characters in society, since there is no standard to judge – or at least not *absolutely* – as to which is better. And indeed Oakeshott goes further, welcoming such a situation, praising the individual who 'is disinclined to be unnerved because there are other . . . [moral] languages to which he cannot readily relate his own' (Oakeshott 1975: 81; see also 54). Unlike Aristotle, in other words, Oakeshott posits, and indeed advocates a fairly robust form of moral pluralism, associating this with modernity.

Furthermore, this commitment to moral pluralism and individualism is confirmed by Oakeshott's analysis of what he sees as the other vital aspect of morality, which he refers to as 'self-enactment'. This does not refer to the way in which Oakeshott has conceived of morality up to this point – namely as the examination of how individuals pursue particular satisfactions by choosing particular actions (or 'disclose' themselves, to use his terminology) – but instead to the 'sentiments' in which they perform such actions. These 'sentiments', Oakeshott maintains, are – analytically at least – entirely distinct from the nature of the actions being performed,[41] and, as such, offer at least a partial means of escaping the inevitable frustrations and disappointments of 'self-disclosure' (Oakeshott 1975: 73), by allowing an agent to cultivate a particular attitude to the world which is not dependent on his pursuit of satisfactions being successful.[42] (Thus an agent can, for example, choose to perform their actions in an attitude of compassion, regret or hatred, the choice being [analytically at least] entirely independent of the actions themselves.) It is true that such an escape can never be total, so that even the attempt at transcending the world's vicissitudes that Oakeshott regards as most successful, namely religion, can never fully succeed. And equally, just as in the case of 'self-disclosure', it is clear that Oakeshott does not mean to suggest that agents can develop purely private, subjective ways of looking at the world – just as with 'self-disclosure', their conceptualizations can be understood by others, since they are inevitably, if perhaps less obviously, the product of a common language and tradition. Nevertheless, what ultimately strikes one when considering 'self-enactment' is once again how individualist Oakeshott's position is: he presents us with no means of judging which kinds of 'self-enactments' are better, and indeed seems to think any kind of judgment of others' self-enactments are a mistake. Rather, he seems to advocate an accepting, perhaps even 'poetic' approach to other individuals' sentiments 'not "judging" them (as we sometimes have to judge their self-disclosures), but contemplating them with admiration, with reserve, or with indulgence' (Oakeshott 1975: 77). Once again therefore, Oakeshott's supposedly neutral philosophical analysis on closer inspection reveals a profound commitment to pluralist individualism – the idea that there can be a genuinely common end for all individuals in modernity is ruled out absolutely.

The civil condition

Having established how he believes we should understand the nature of human behaviour in modernity, stressing its plurality above all, in the second essay of *On Human Conduct*, Oakeshott puts forward an account of the state that he believes can respect this plurality, so that the individuals within a state can act as freely as possible. In doing so, Oakeshott continues to maintain that he is merely putting forward a possible way of analysing the modern European state, an 'ideal character', rather than a normative argument for how the state *should* be organized, but the further one proceeds through the second essay of *On Human Conduct*, the harder it is to take this at face value. At the very least it seems clear that, if one finds Oakeshott's account of the nature of human behaviour convincing, then he believes we should find his account of the modern state attractive. By contrast, Oakeshott's claim that we are unlikely to find such a state ever existing in pure form in practice is much easier to take seriously – since (he claims) states will always to some extent be organized around common goals – but this seems to be more a matter of unavoidable regret, as far as Oakeshott is concerned, rather than something to be welcomed. To investigate Oakeshott's favoured conception of the state, which he labels 'civil association', we will first examine how he differentiates this from other kinds of state, before exploring his identification of it as a form of 'moral practice', and more widely how he conceives of the 'rule of law'.

First, therefore, Oakeshott seeks to distinguish 'civil association' from what he sees as its main alternative, which he calls 'enterprise association'.[43] The crucial difference between the two is that 'civil association' merely establishes a particular kind of relationship between agents, rather than being organized to pursue any kind of common purpose, whereas it is precisely the point of 'enterprise association' to subordinate all other concerns to the pursuance of one particular end.

This is not to say that Oakeshott regards the mode of 'enterprise association' as inherently reprehensible, as long as the participants have a choice as to whether to join a group organized in this way or not, it is clearly the best method of organization when seeking an instrumental goal. But he is emphatic that it is utterly inappropriate when it comes to organizing the state, given his strong emphasis on the diversity of individuals within a society, since by definition a state's laws are compulsory and cannot be accepted or rejected through individual choice. Given that in other words, as we have seen, Oakeshott takes it as axiomatic that individuals in modernity necessarily pursue incommensurable satisfactions, it cannot be legitimate to organize the state around the pursuance of one 'common good', since no such genuinely 'common good' exists.[44] And he meets the obvious objection to this position, namely that all modern states pursue at least basic common ends such as peace and security by controversially denying that these are substantive goals at all – rather, he claims, they represent purely formal conditions that must pertain for a state to continue to exist at all.[45]

Having rejected 'enterprise association' as a possible model for how to organize the state, Oakeshott proceeds to try to specify more exactly what 'civil association' consists of. In doing so, he does not attempt to produce a full description of the workings of the state, since he declines to discuss several aspects of it that other theorists would see as crucial – such as a full description of its political institutions (as found in Hegel's *Philosophy of Right*, for example), of its economy or of how it should relate to other states. Instead, in describing 'civil association' what Oakeshott offers is an attempt to describe (or at least sketch) how law should operate in order to safeguard the freedom of individuals, and to respect their diversity in a modern state, also providing some guidance on how law should relate to morality. Crucial to his case is to argue that essentially 'civil association' should be identified as a type of moral practice – in other words a relationship that is learned practically, which qualifies rather than prescribes the actions of agents affected by it and which is not (as we have established) designed to aim at any particular end. As such, Oakeshott maintains, it can therefore be fruitfully compared to a vernacular language, distinct from other such 'languages' like those of 'love' or 'rivalry', with which it can nevertheless still coexist. But, Oakeshott argues, it also importantly differs from these other 'languages', and in two ways. First, if recognized at all, the 'language' of civility has a particular importance in relating agents, since it is in some sense the guarantor of civilization – and hence, where acknowledged at all, 'there is no situation *inter homines* to which it cannot relate' (Oakeshott 1975: 123), so that 'of the many different kinds of consideration . . . an agent may acknowledge in his performances, those which belong to an art of civil relationship may properly occupy a large or a small part of his attention, but they will rarely be absent and never wholly irrelevant' (Oakeshott 1975: 124). And, second, more specifically, civil association differs from many other moral practices in essentially consisting of a system of rules, this being a concept that is crucial to Oakeshott's theory of civil association, and which he therefore spends some time in clarifying.

How then should rules be defined, according to Oakeshott? Essentially, he argues that they have three crucial features, all of which distinguish them sharply from commands, which Oakeshott rejects as a basis for law under any circumstances. First, he argues that rules must be distinguished from 'theorems', since they are not pieces of advice, to be evaluated in terms of their desirability, but are rather intrinsically *authoritative* in nature. The obligation to obey rules, in other words, cannot be linked to how sensible the rule in question is, or the consequences of obeying (or not obeying) them; rather it is intrinsic to the very concept of a rule. Second, unlike a command, which demands the performance of one particular action from an assignable agent on an individual basis, a rule is by definition general and abstract in nature. It cannot be 'used up' in any one performance, but instead both exist in advance of any particular situation, and, even after application 'remains 'standing' for unknown future occasions' (Oakeshott 1975: 127).[46] Genuinely to qualify as a rule, in other words, it must apply to all in the association equally, making no discrimination according to any particular contingent circumstances. Finally, however, rules do not prescribe particular courses of action in detail – they do not 'enjoin, prohibit, or warrant substantive actions or utterances; they cannot tell agents what to do or to say' (Oakeshott 1975: 129). Rather, Oakeshott argues, being a moral practice, rules by definition qualify performances adverbially – so that to obey a rule is necessarily to engage in an act of interpretation, not to perform a particular action. To argue otherwise is to misunderstand the concept of what a rule is.

Having identified that civil association is a form of moral practice essentially based upon rules, Oakeshott then proceeds to try and specify the nature of the association further. By definition, as a 'civil', as opposed to 'enterprise' association, those within it – the 'cives' as Oakeshott calls them – are related purely through the rules involved, rather than in terms of any extrinsic purpose. As such, Oakeshott argues, in order for the association to function properly at all, they must be related not simply in terms of the rules themselves, but also in terms of a *recognition* of the authority of those rules. As already stated, by this he does not mean that the laws must be recognized as desirable for any particular reason – as being 'just', for example – or because they are likely to be enforced.[47] Rather, the system of laws governing civil association – or 'lex' as Oakeshott calls it – must be recognized as authoritative purely through the laws in question being accepted as legitimately passed, by being the result of a valid procedure. This obviously implies that there are certain criteria which must be followed if laws are to be valid, which Oakeshott specifies (or at least sketches) in a long footnote – demanding that laws must not be arbitrary, secret, retroactive or in hock to special interests; that judicial proceedings must be independent and that there must be no penalties without specific offences, to name but the most important (Oakeshott 1975: 153 n. 1). But although Oakeshott believes these criteria to be vital, it is important not to exaggerate how systematic they are – the way laws are related to one another will always remain to some extent imprecise, underdetermined, slightly ramshackle. It is false, in other words, he believes, to suggest that one can derive universal criteria for recognizing laws from any other source – whether this be from a single rule of recognition, or, more ambitiously, from one fundamental, unquestionable norm from which all the other laws obtain their authority.[48] The best one can do is to check that individual laws have been correctly passed, Oakeshott argues, and, if so to recognize their authority accordingly.

Insofar as 'lex' is considered solely in terms of the authority it has, Oakeshott argues, it can never be a threat to individual freedom, since it neither requires individuals to perform particular actions, nor forbids them from doing so, but (as a moral practice) merely qualifies adverbially the actions that citizens choose to perform. Moreover, because the authority that 'lex' has is not dependent on the approval of the citizens it affects, by definition it cannot be something that is able to be the focus of their disapproval – all it does is to provide a framework in which such citizens are able to make their particular choices. But it is also important to stress that this does not exhaust the ways in which 'lex' can be considered. For although Oakeshott is adamant that what make laws authoritative must not be confused with other ways of considering them, this does not preclude considering how desirable laws are, any more than it precludes the activities of 'adjudication' – namely the interpretation of law in particular cases – or of 'ruling' – namely the activity of enforcing law through and enforcing sanctions to do so. (Indeed, both of the latter activities are in fact not merely *possible* but *necessary*, as far as Oakeshott is concerned, given the general and abstract nature of laws passed in 'civil association'.) This important (but limited) activity is what Oakeshott defines as 'politics', and he is insistent that, in order to be compatible with the concept of 'civil association', it must necessarily be a much more modest engagement than it is often believed to be. For since, by definition, a 'civil association' cannot pursue one substantive end without violating the liberty of the citizens within it – even if this (for example) merely consists in upholding one overarching criterion for distributive justice over another – the function of 'politics' must inevitably be a fairly limited one, as far as Oakeshott is concerned.

What then does Oakeshott consider the true role of 'politics' to be? Essentially he argues that it must consist of a procedure to consider how desirable and just laws within civil association are, taking each issue as it arises on a case-by-case basis, eschewing any 'final solution' to political problems. For, just as in his earlier work, he continues to argue that, such is the concrete and plural complexity of political life, it is impossible to grasp the nature of society as a whole, not least because any 'solution' to one particular problem will almost inevitably bring other tensions within society to the surface (Oakeshott 1975: 173) – so that political principles are inadequate as a guide for political action, being necessarily one-sided abstractions, which require further interpretation in practice. (Thus theories of natural law, for example, Oakeshott argues, to take one of the most distinguished sources of political principle, are too vaguely formulated to provide help in practice – even if, as often occurs, they are formulated into more specific political precepts, such a bill of rights or a fundamental norm.) However, Oakeshott still believes it is possible to make judgments about how moral particular laws are, rejecting the position of legal positivists who suggest that there is an absolute split between law and morality. Such judgments will necessarily be contentious and subject to dispute, since they will be historically derived, rather than deduced from absolute truths, but nevertheless (he believes) can escape the fate of being purely arbitrary. In some manner they will be related to the morality of modern society as a whole, and beyond this premise Oakeshott is either unwilling or believes it impossible to analyse. He seems to take it as axiomatic that in order to function at all, a society cannot be so morally divided that it is incapable of making moral judgments about its laws. In his defence, it should be stated that this is far from being an unreasonable contention, especially since Oakeshott is very clear that we are likely to have far fewer moral judgments in common about what can be imposed by law than more generally in society. Nevertheless Oakeshott's intuition that law and morality must be related, albeit imperfectly and obliquely, remains rather tantalizing, since he declines to discuss the matter further, leaving only a sketch. Ultimately, he believes, these are questions that must be resolved in practice.

On History

Having delineated the main elements of Oakeshott's mature political theory, as put forward in *On Human Conduct*, it remains for us to examine his philosophy of history, the most detailed account of which is to be found in Oakeshott's other major later work *On History* (though Oakeshott's account of the mode remains essentially the same throughout his career). Part of the reason for doing this is simply that this fills a gap in our account of Oakeshott's work, since 'History' Oakeshott believes, is one of the most sophisticated ways that human beings have developed in modernity to understand the world in which they live.[49] As such, like 'Science' or 'Poetry', Oakeshott maintains, it offers a theoretical escape from the interminable demands of 'Practice', of 'the deadliness of doing', by helping us to interpret human actions in a sophisticated and satisfying way, despite its ultimate limitations. But beyond this, there is also a more immediate reason to investigate Oakeshott's historical method, namely that it reveals how he thinks we should theorize about individual examples of human conduct, and hence connects very directly with his argument in *On Human Conduct* itself. For if his account of 'human conduct' tells us how he believes that we should understand human behaviour in general, Oakeshott believes that more specific instances of it should be understood historically, as the outcome of past events – so that, as he puts it himself, 'the theoretical understanding of a substantive action or utterance is . . . a "historical" understanding' (Oakeshott 1975: 105).

What then does it mean to understand human conduct 'historically', according to Oakeshott? Essentially he argues that 'History' consists of the attempt to construct a past that has not survived through the interrogation of present evidence, so that, following Hegel, he dismisses the idea that the aim of historical study is merely to catalogue or recollect past events as they actually happened. Part of the reason for this is simply that we lack the required evidence to be able to do this – since the surviving evidence we have is both incomplete and does not (in any case) necessarily tell us what we want to know about the past. But, more particularly, it is because by definition 'History', as a developed mode of understanding, necessarily involves more organization of the material in question than mere cataloguing or recollecting – although, perhaps paradoxically, a crucial part of this 'organisation' in fact entails letting alone past events (having been constructed) to speak for themselves. Acting as an historian, in other words, not only requires 'thought', the subscription to certain key postulates just as other modes do, but it also involves respecting the intrinsic nature of past events, so that no merely artificial, external structure is imposed from outside to make sense of them. And as such, Oakeshott argues, certain approaches to the past that have become popular – notably the practical and the scientific – are ruled out because they do not respect this criterion. Thus the practical approach to the past is inappropriate because it assumes a past full of useful precedents for dealing with the present, rather than a problematic past that has to be constructed and explored – and indeed, in its strongest form, denies the very possibility of disinterested historical inquiry by claiming that both the nature and content of historical study will inevitably be dictated by present concerns.[50] And equally a scientific approach is inappropriate, for analogous reasons. For even if, he argues, we reject the idea that history can be understood as the result of fully determined general causal laws – which are, according to Oakeshott, by definition necessarily inadequate to understand human conduct – and instead content ourselves with trying to make history more intelligible through the use of empirically falsifiable causal laws, we are inevitably having to make certain dubious assumptions about the past in order for this to be possible. In particular, Oakeshott argues, it has to be assumed that past events are 'already described and understood kinds of happenings', lacking 'only deductive proof of their occurrence', rather than occurrences which it is the job of the historian to explain – since otherwise no such causal link could be hypothesized. And closely related to this is the assumption that present evidence gives us an unproblematic knowledge of past events, an account of 'given' events which require explanation – as opposed to contested and only partially understood historical happenings. But both assumptions, he maintains, are almost self-evidently false since past events are not 'givens' but can only be constructed with difficulty, and furthermore remain contested. Once again, a purely artificial structure is being imposed.

If such accounts are to be rejected, according to Oakeshott, how then should the historian attempt to analyse the past? Essentially, he conceives of it as a fairly modest engagement, which tries to give some coherence to it, rather than one that tries to give a complete and total account of the past – as Hegel, most famously, had aspired to do.[51] Furthermore, although he does not rule them out as illegitimate, Oakeshott is wary of historical accounts that try and explain the past in terms of agents subscribing to traditions or 'practices', since, as we have seen, such practices are constantly in flux, and hence leave behind rather elusive clues to their nature, rather than evidence that is easy to interpret. (As Oakeshott puts it, they should be regarded not as 'stable compositions of easily recognized characteristics', but rather as 'footprints left behind by agents responding to their emergent situations . . . [which] are only somewhat less evanescent than the transactions in which they emerged' [Oakeshott 1975: 100].) Moreover, as we would expect, although Oakeshott thinks that identifying an historical event as being the illustration of a 'practice' will certainly identify something important about it, it does not usually capture what is most significant about it. This is that (as human conduct) it is the result of contingent, but intelligent, responses by individual agents.[52] As such, Oakeshott argues, what the historian instead needs to do is gradually construct an account of historical events, using the limited evidence – or 'survivals' – that he has at his disposal, which views these events as both the result of particular individual decisions, and yet also as part of a longer process of historical continuity and change.

To do this in practice, Oakeshott argues that historians have to proceed carefully and methodically. First, they must use the 'survivals' at their disposal to try to work out the circumstances in which such pieces of evidence came into existence 'to understand performances recognized as survivals in terms of the transactional relationship which constitute their characters as performances' (Oakeshott 1983: 51), as Oakeshott puts it. This is a difficult task, not only because the answer to this question will vary according to the precise historical question being asked, but also because (Oakeshott stresses) the survivals that a historian has to work with tend to be both damaged and incomplete, so that 'an historical enquiry begins . . . with a present of performances which have survived, which speak, but which do not address themselves to the questions an historian is concerned to answer' (Oakeshott 1983: 56). (As such, Oakeshott warns against using 'survivals' more ambitiously as evidence of past acts, since usually they do not provide reliable testimony about them – rather the reverse, in fact, he believes.) Second, having done their best to determine how 'survivals' came into being, historians then need to question them more critically, to try and construct historical 'occurrences' that took place, an 'occurrence' being defined as something that is 'not itself an artefact . . . which has survived, nor a performance, but [rather] the net outcome of divergent and perhaps conflicting performances' (Oakeshott 1983: 57). From there, Oakeshott claims, historians can then extend such a process to construct historical 'situations', which are more developed versions of 'occurrences', being defined as coherent structures of 'mutually and conceptually related occurrences abstracted from all that may have been going on there' (Oakeshott 1983: 59). (Some examples of these include 'the civilization of Renaissance Italy', 'the Scottish Enlightenment' and 'Jeffersonian democracy'.) Critically, these 'situations' are very much something that an historian has constructed, and hence can vary according to the historical question asked, they are not purely subjective: the evidence itself provides constraints about what can reasonably be inferred about the past. For although the evidence that can be used to construct such 'situations' (namely 'survivals') does not have an 'exclusive reference', and hence is 'eligible to be drawn upon in constructing a variety of historical situations', this does not mean that all interpretations are equally good.

To understand past occurrences as historical 'situations', then, according to Oakeshott, is certainly to have attained quite a sophisticated level of understanding. But it is not sufficient for a genuinely *historical* understanding of the past, since it is too static – it does not properly explain how such 'situations' *happen*. To achieve this, the situations must be transformed into historical 'events', by placing them in a genuinely dynamic, diachronic sequence, and such an operation must be done carefully or otherwise the historian will go awry. For, Oakeshott argues, it is not enough simply to start with a particular 'situation' that has to be explained, and then try to analyse it by looking at its direct antecedents, since this is to give the situation an unwarranted priority over other situations, by regarding it as a 'given', something static to be explained. Rather, the historian must be careful to give sufficient weight to what Oakeshott calls 'the circumstantial confluence of vicissitudes' that brought this about – so that the historical situation being analysed must be regarded as just as transformable as all the others in play. (Thus, if we seek to explain the abolition of the British slave trade, to cite Oakeshott's example, then rather than merely looking at the history of the trade and the activities of its opponents, we must be careful to examine the immediate contingencies that led to this event [Oakeshott: 1983: 69–70].) And the result of this procedure is that instead of aiming to explain relative static historical entities such as 'the condition of England in 1685', the historian ends up producing a much more dynamic account, seeking instead to explain how historical 'events' occur as part of a narrative sequence.

If, then, the implication of Oakeshott's argument is that the historian should aim to produce a narrative of events, rather than merely trying to explain static historical situations, this logically raises the question of how these events should be related to one another. A key characteristic of this relationship, Oakeshott argues, is that it 'enhances the intelligibility of the . . . [events] concerned' – a requirement which rules out a relationship that simply juxtaposes events in a purely factual manner or merely 'correlates' events 'in terms of likenesses or arbitrarily chosen characteristics', since this only relates events formally, rather than shedding any further light on them (Oakeshott 1983: 78). Conversely, however, as we have seen already, Oakeshott also stresses that it is important that the historian does not try and make sense of past events by imposing a purely external structure on them – which rules out any attempts to relate them in organic, teleological, evolutionary or mechanical terms, or, more widely, in terms of the functional dependence of a relationship of 'implication and entailment' or analogically (Oakeshott 1983: 78–100). Instead, Oakeshott argues, the historian should attempt to relate historical events together 'contingently', by which he means purely 'in terms of their dependent connections with other such occurrences', so that prior events are to be regarded as the condition for subsequent ones – but only so that the sequence of events is rendered more intelligible through their association, not that the relationship is causal or systematic. Crucially, Oakeshott maintains, there is no necessity to this relationship between events; on the contrary, there is no reason why other prior events cannot equally be significantly related to subsequent ones – indeed, this is likely to be necessary if a different historical question is being answered (Oakeshott 1975: 94–5). Equally, espousing this position does not mean that every juxtaposition of events is permitted, since not all such juxtapositions will be meaningful – the content of the prior event must in some way be related to the subsequent. To use Oakeshott's own analogy, the act of producing a passage of contingent events should be regarded as similar to the construction of a dry stone wall. On the one hand, 'the stones . . . which compose the wall . . . [namely] the antecedent events . . . [and] subsequent event[s] . . . are joined and held together, not by mortar, but in terms of their shapes'. But on the other, Oakeshott insists, 'the wall . . . has no premeditated design; it is what its components, in touching, constitute' (Oakeshott 1983: 102).

Finally, Oakeshott maintains, one further important consequence of this position is that it necessitates adopting a particular view of historical change. Essentially he argues that since the only criterion for building up a meaningful passage of historical 'events' is their own appropriateness and intelligibility with reference to one another, what guarantees the meaningfulness of a passage of changing historical events is, paradoxically, their inherent continuity. Because each event cannot be analysed as a complete change from the previous one in other words – since, Oakeshott argues, this is logically incoherent – the very meaningfulness of a given passage of events must be found in what actually guarantees its shape – in short, in its continuity (Oakeshott 1983: 108). Since Oakeshott takes it as axiomatic that no pattern can be imposed on the past in advance, however, it follows that conversely whatever 'continuity' there is in an historical narrative must be provided by the selection of historical events themselves – not from any particular fixed point in the narrative or from a more general structure. As Oakeshott puts it himself: Historical change is 'to be distinguished from some changeless item in the situation, from an enduring purpose or end to be realized and from the normalities of the "law" of a process of change'. Rather, we must seek continuity 'in some intrinsic quality of the assemblage itself, or else confess that an historical past is no more than a tissue of fortuitous conjunctions' (Oakeshott 1983: 113–14). Thus no criteria for how we view particular historical changes, Oakeshott maintains, can be established in advance: they will be purely a produce of the historical question being asked, and the events chosen. And more generally this is quite a good summary of Oakeshott's conception of history in general – his constant theme is that any coherence in an historical narrative must come from the events themselves, nowhere else.

Conclusion

What emerges, then, from this exploration of the major parts of Oakeshott's work? Above all, what becomes clear is how strong a defender of modernity he is. For, despite some irritation with the nature of modern life which shows itself in particular in some of his middle-period essays, and his still-common reputation as the scourge of the Enlightenment, Oakeshott emerges as essentially an upholder of modern pluralism, eschewing any romanticism concerning the medieval period. This shows itself on both theoretical and practical levels. At a theoretical level, he was keen to uphold the value of certain kinds of non-philosophical ways of understanding the world, both against the claims of each other, but more particularly against the claims of practice. These developed 'modes' of experience – namely history, science and poetry – represented, for Oakeshott, a hard-won escape from doing (which he saw as a 'deadly thing') (Oakeshott 2004: 309), and he was insistent they should be defended at all costs as a major achievement. On a more practical level, as we have seen, Oakeshott was also a strong defender of pluralist individualism. While accepting that societies are bound together by common tradition, in other words, for Oakeshott what was exciting about modernity is that (at least in Europe) mankind has learned – by and large – to conceptualize itself primarily in terms of individualism, rather than in terms of collective, communal organization. This has opened the way for mankind to enjoy a freedom little known before the onset of modernity, provided the right kind of state can be maintained to uphold such freedom – hence Oakeshott's attempt to provide one in 'The Civil Condition' in *On Human Conduct*. None of this, of course, is to suggest that Oakeshott's work is perfect. There remain at the very least distinct omissions in his political theory – notably concerning the economy, international law and even over how precisely he defines the institutions that should defend the 'rule of law'. And philosophically, the status of the modes remains problematic: can they really be *quite* as incommensurable as Oakeshott claims? But at the very least it seems reasonable to claim that Oakeshott emerges from this analysis as much more worth engaging with than has often been claimed. In subsequent chapters we will try to come to an assessment concerning his work, both by attempting to set him more firmly into a post-war intellectual context, and by trying to set the vexed question of whether Oakeshott is best seen as a 'conservative' or a 'liberal' in appropriate historical context.

Chapter 3

The Reception of Michael Oakeshott's Thought

Having explored the nature of Oakeshott's life and thought in the first two chapters, we can now proceed to examine the reception of his work, assessing his impact both on his contemporaries and beyond. Doing so, however, is not a straightforward task, since Oakeshott's work, at least until recently, has often been analysed in rather unsatisfactory terms, at best examined in discrete, separable parts, and at worst being (at least partially) misinterpreted. As we saw in the previous chapter, this is partly explained by the nature of the work that Oakeshott published in his lifetime, so that despite the underlying unity in his thought, to a casual observer he appeared to be addressing quite separate topics in his major books. Thus he seemed to lurch from a concern with Idealist epistemology in *Experience and Its Modes*, to a focus on the virtues of tradition in *Rationalism in Politics and Other Essays*, later examining the kind of state that he believed could guarantee individual freedom in modernity in *On Human Conduct*, before trying to codify how one should investigate the past in *On History and Other Essays*. But this problem has also been exacerbated by three other factors, which have tended to ensure that Oakeshott's work did not get a fair hearing, and which contributed to commentators on his work feeling somewhat baffled.

First, the style that Oakeshott used to write his major works tended to be highly idiosyncratic, introducing technical terms without full explanation, and using ordinary vocabulary in unusual ways, much to the puzzlement of at least some of his readers. Thus *Experience and Its Modes* demanded a knowledge of the specifics of Idealist vocabulary,[1] *On Human Conduct* introduced a whole phalanx of new terms (both in English and Latin) in an attempt to avoid ambiguity – such as 'goings-on', 'self-disclosure', '*lex*' and '*respublica*' to name but a few[2] – while even the superficially easier *Rationalism in Politics* conceals important ambiguities in its rather imprecise use of critical terms like 'self', 'practical knowledge' and 'tradition', which tend to raise serious questions once the enjoyment of Oakeshott's breezy style here has faded.[3] Moreover, Oakeshott makes little effort to clarify the way in which he changes his use of critical terms throughout his work – his rather cavalier use of the word 'practice' causing particular trouble.[4] Second, Oakeshott's arguments are difficult to compare to those of other thinkers directly, since even at his most polemical, as he frequently is in *Rationalism in Politics*, Oakeshott rarely takes issue with his contemporaries' views directly, in general preferring instead to take the canonic thinkers of the Western philosophical tradition (such as Aristotle, Bacon, Descartes and Spinoza) as his interlocutors – rather than engaging directly with (for example) Laski, Arendt, Hayek or Berlin.[5] Furthermore, in much of his work, and in *On Human Conduct* above all, Oakeshott's preference is as much to detail his own position as it is to take issue with others', so that those critics who complain his work proceeds by assertion rather than argument have a certain justice on their side – an impression reinforced by Oakeshott's refusal to countenance the conventional academic support-structure of footnotes and bibliography.⁶ Finally, Oakeshott's work proved difficult to set in a more immediate historical context because he was wary of drawing practical implications from his theoretical conclusions, even in interviews (when he gave them) or off the cuff. (Infamously, for example, when asked whether Britain should remain a member of the European Economic Community, as it then was, at the time of the referendum in 1975, Oakeshott replied that he did 'not find it necessary to hold opinions on such matters' [see Boucher 1991: 718].) And more generally, Oakeshott tended to eschew any potential role as a 'public intellectual',⁷ preferring to stick to communicating with a more severely academic audience, rather than offering prescriptive advice. Despite undoubtedly having an impact on the way politics and history have been studied in Britain, therefore, Oakeshott's more immediate political impact has been fairly minimal.⁸

In these circumstances, rather than exploring commentators' immediate reactions to Oakeshott's work in detail – since although these sometimes hit the mark, more often than not they simply represent misunderstandings of Oakeshott's position⁹ – what I propose to do here is to try and set his work in some contexts that help to make better sense of his thinking. To understand the 'reception' of Oakeshott's thought, in other words, we need both to understand the general intellectual climate in which he was writing, and his specific intentions better. First, for example, it is certainly worth noting that, rather than viewing *Experience and Its Modes* as simply a culmination of Oakeshott's youthful preoccupation with trying to identify the correct relationship between philosophy, poetry and other modes,¹⁰ the work probably also represents a response to an important Idealist work of the period – namely R. G. Collingwood's *Speculum Mentis* (1924). As we have seen already, this book argued that the major modes of experience are arranged in a hierarchy, so that art, religion, science and history were cumulatively exposed as inadequate – a position explicitly rejected by Oakeshott – but it also put forward two further theses. For Collingwood also claimed that theoretical endeavours are always intimately related to practice, so that 'all thought exists for the sake of action' (Collingwood 1924: 15), and secondly that the diversity of the types of knowledge in modernity is intrinsically harmful, having destroyed the unity of knowledge that existed in the medieval period, where 'there was a general interpretation of the various activities of the mind, in which each was influenced by all' (Collingwood 1924: 27). Clearly *Experience and Its Modes* sets out a pointedly opposed position to this, despite the common Idealist background that Oakeshott and Collingwood share, arguing that although 'thinking is at first associated with an extraneous desire for action', nevertheless 'we must learn not to follow the philosophers upon these holiday excursions' (Oakeshott 1933: 1), and further insisting that each (modern) mode of experience is valuable in itself. And more widely, on a more political level, Oakeshott's insistence on the desirability of modern individualism in his later work, on the basis that this allows humans to be freer than they were in earlier periods, is surely at least partly a riposte to Collingwood's hierarchical vision (as laid out in *Speculum Mentis*). This upheld the importance of guilds, churches and the feudal hierarchy, on the basis that within these institutions an individual 'found a place where he was wanted, work for him to do [and] a market for his wards', so that 'he could devote himself to fulfilling the duties assigned him by his station in that great organism within which he found himself lodged' (Collingwood 1924: 23); modern individualism by contrast, offered only illusory liberty and an unhappy, divided self-absorbed consciousness. If there were certainly other influences playing their role in causing Oakeshott to advocate modern individualist pluralism, there seems little doubt that a repudiation of Collingwood's rather romanticized vision of the medieval period was also one of Oakeshott's aims.

However, although the dispute with Collingwood provides us with an important context for understanding what Oakeshott was trying to do in his work, especially in his earlier pieces of writing, probably the most important context for understanding most of Oakeshott's arguments is the post-war period. Partly, this is simply because it is the period when Oakeshott's writings had most impact, but it is also because it is arguably the time when Oakeshott was most directly reacting to other thinkers, whether they be logical positivists, ordinary language philosophers or Cold War liberals – notwithstanding a continuing reluctance to refer to any of them by name – and we will examine his relationship with each of these groups in turn.

It is certainly worth remarking that Oakeshott's arguments in this period had more in common with some of the post-war positivists' than has often been noticed, despite this at first sight appearing highly counter-intuitive. Obviously there were a wide variety of positivist arguments being put forward in this period, and Oakeshott's position certainly differed markedly from some of them. Thus in particular, as we have seen, he was strongly resistant to the idea that human conduct can only be satisfactorily explained as the result of mechanical processes, whether natural or social, arguing that natural science does not provide the only paradigm for gaining knowledge of the world. As such, he argued against those who maintained that human conduct was in reality causally determined – such as the nineteenth-century positivists J. S. Mill and Herbert Spencer, for example[11] – as well as those twentieth-century positivists (like A. J. Ayer) who, while more circumspect, argued that such a possibility could not be ruled out (Ayer 1967). And furthermore, as we seen, although as an idealist more sympathetic to those who claimed (like Ernst Mach) that genuine scientific method consists of a particular way of *describing* (natural or social) occurrences that claims nothing about actual causal connections in *reality*, as a pluralist, Oakeshott rejects the idea that scientific description is the only possible candidate as a way of understanding (for more, see Mach 1914; Bradley 1971). Instead, as we have seen, he believes that there is a plurality of equally good modes of understanding the world, where science is a plausible candidate for understanding particular phenomena, but far from being the only possible one.

However, having said all this, there are nevertheless some interesting parallels to be drawn between Oakeshott's middle-period work and that of T. D. Weldon, a positivist philosopher, whose work on the nature of political philosophy and of politics more generally was highly influential in the 1940s and 1950s. Certainly, they were far from in total agreement. As he did with other positivists, Oakeshott differed with Weldon over the latter's advocacy of the verification principle – namely the idea that unless statements could be empirically verified (or alternatively were beyond doubt) they were meaningless – since this was once again to imply that there was only one genuine language that could be used to describe the world. But despite this, to the extent that he argues – in such well-known works from the 1940s and 1950s as *States and Morals* (1946) and *The Vocabulary of Politics* (1953) – that philosophy is unable to aid practical decisions his work is strongly reminiscent of that of Oakeshott's in the same era; indeed, in this respect the arguments of the two are more or less identical. Thus for Weldon, just as for Oakeshott, all philosophizing can do is to clarify conceptual ambiguities that underlie our practical activities, to resolve second-order problems that are (as Weldon puts it) generated by the language in which facts are described and explained (Weldon 1953: 22). What it cannot do, is to recommend substantive courses of action since the abstract conclusions provided by philosophy are too generalized to provide appropriate knowledge for the decisions that individuals have to make in practice.[12] But this does not mean, for Weldon any more than Oakeshott, that such decisions are made on a purely subjective basis – rather, he believes, it means that individuals have to rely instead on the common experience that is provided by society, so that although the reasons for their practical decisions cannot be proved deductively, they can nevertheless be justified on a non-subjective basis. (Thus, to take Weldon's example, the way in which a committee makes decisions about the suitability of individual candidates before them is open to rational discussion and disagreement, since although its criteria – such as honesty, assiduity, intelligence, etc – will be, on their own, too abstract to help them do this, they can nevertheless be more or less satisfactorily applied to individual cases, and hence fruitfully and rationally discussed [Weldon 1953: 151–6].) And for both Weldon and Oakeshott, since political decisions are essentially practical, they should be made on this basis, rather than by – primarily at least – making reference to philosophical analysis. Overall therefore, notwithstanding some remaining differences – not least over the precise way in which Weldon and Oakeshott justify their division between philosophy and practice[13] – on this point at least Oakeshott's position in this period is similar to Weldon's.

Clearly then, there are some similarities between Oakeshott's position and that of Weldon's positivism, particularly over the division between philosophy and practice. Arguably even more striking, however, in the 1950s and later, are the parallels between Oakeshott's arguments and those of the ordinary language philosophers – especially over their hostility to causal explanations, and more generally over how to theorize about social practices. In particular, Oakeshott's arguments seem to resemble those of Peter Winch, who was perhaps the most explicit amongst ordinary language philosophers in seeking to draw out the implications of that philosophical position for the social sciences (and for sociology in particular), most notably in his well-known book *The Idea of a Social Science and Its Relation to Philosophy* (1958). In that work, Winch sought to examine how the arguments of the ordinary language philosophers' main inspirer, namely Wittgenstein, can be used to provide an appropriate methodology for understanding human conduct, stressing in particular Wittgenstein's emphasis on the importance of seeing meaningful human behaviour as being governed by 'rules'.[14] This led him to espouse three arguments which closely resemble Oakeshott's position in this area.

First, closely resembling Oakeshott's arguments concerning 'practices', as put forward in *On Human Conduct*, and explicitly borrowing from Wittgenstein's argument that the meaning of linguistic utterances in particular, but also of human actions more generally, can only be understood successfully if they are regarded as the result of conventions, rather than of an intentional mental process, Winch insists that human conduct should be understood in terms of 'rules'.

By this, what he means to suggest is that an agent's actions will only be meaningful if they constitute a response that conforms to a convention (or 'rule') that other agents around him or her can recognize, and that, furthermore, to interpret these actions successfully a sociologist must understand the particular rule that the agent in question is following – otherwise the interpretation will at best go awry, and at worst be meaningless. Thus, for example, one can only understand Chaucer's Troilus properly if one understands the rules that underlie courtly love (Winch 1958: 82) – just as for Oakeshott, one may only be able to understand the actions of a Thelemite monk if one understands the 'practice' of Augustinian rule that he is following (Oakeshott 1975: 78).[15]

Second, Winch argues, since rules are not simply conventions that are followed blindly, but are rather applied intelligently by agents in particular situations, it necessarily follows that to understand the application of a given rule correctly we need to understand how an agent is conceptualizing it – rules are not entities that are simply external to agents, in other words. As such, he argues – just as Oakeshott does throughout his work – this means that trying to explain human behaviour causally is a mistaken enterprise, since inevitably this will deny that an agent's own understanding of their situation is relevant – instead a causal explanation seeks to impose external concepts from without, in the hope of detecting (potentially quantifiable) processes. And this is the case, Winch argues (again like Oakeshott), whether interpreters are trying to explain an agent's conduct with reference to either unconscious impulses or external social forces – since in neither case is the sociologist respecting the way agents understand themselves. (Thus he specifically takes aim against Emile Durkheim's claim that 'social life should be explained, not by the notions of those who participate in it, but by more profound causes which are unperceived by consciousness' [Winch 1958: 23–4], and accepts Freudian analyses of patients' symptoms only insofar as the patients themselves are prepared to accept the concepts being proffered to them by their therapists – and not as causal hypotheses [Winch 1958: 48].[16])

Finally, again following on from the premise that rules (properly so-called) and by extension traditions more generally are not simply conventions that can be mechanically applied, Winch stresses the importance of some reflection in the process of applying rules, his position again closely resembling Oakeshott's. At first sight this seems a rather controversial claim to make, since Winch actually claims, very specifically, that his position is different from Oakeshott's on this point, arguing that the latter's conception of rationality – especially as put forward in 'Rational Conduct' – significantly underestimates the role that reflection can play (as against practical knowledge) (Winch 1958: 62–5). But in fact, since Winch himself constantly stresses the importance of practical know-how, and emphasizes that what his position hinges on is the premise that 'the notion of a principle (or maxim) of conduct and the notion of meaningful action are *interwoven*' (Winch 1958: 63) it becomes clear that the difference is more apparent than real. For as we saw, although Oakeshott may be more radical than most of his contemporaries in insisting that rational abilities are relative to the activity being pursued, nevertheless there is nothing in his argument that precludes the idea that ideas and activities are interwoven. Indeed, on the contrary, following Aristotle, Oakeshott's account of acting rationally is precisely premised on the ability not merely to be able to respond practically to a situation, but to diagnose its nature in the first place – not as two processes, but as one.[17] So Winch's position was closer to Oakeshott's than in fact he claimed.

It is important to note, of course, that the two thinkers' positions are not identical – there are also two key differences between them. In particular, although both Winch and Oakeshott are in a loose sense 'idealist' thinkers, since they both believe that we lack the ability to know the world 'in itself', instead having to content ourselves with a knowledge of it that is mediated, they differ significantly over the cause of that mediation. For Oakeshott, as we have seen, what determines this are the postulates of particular modes which – though they can be more or less consciously held – are ultimately the result of thought, not language. In this sense Oakeshott remains true to his Idealist heritage, since – from Hegel onwards – the Idealists always took it as axiomatic that conscious thought, ultimately at least, had primacy over linguistic expression.[18] For Winch, by contrast, following Wittgenstein, what determines our ability to know things is emphatically language, not any kind of dictates of conscious thought: for him as much as his master, 'the limits of language are the limits of our world' (Wittgenstein 1961: comment 5.6). Second, whereas as we have seen, Oakeshott essentially concurred with Weldon that there is an unbridgeable divide between philosophy and practice, so that philosophical conclusions are more or less useless in a social and political context, for Winch, one of the key problems with the logical positivists was precisely their insistence on this hard and fast distinction. Instead, Winch argued, rather than reducing philosophy to the role of 'under labourer', as Locke had advocated, which limits its role to exploring certain unchanging facts about the world, one should admit that all kinds of practical behaviour could only be pursued relative to a particular philosophical scheme (Winch 1958: 2–7) – thus, for him the 'rules' that practical conduct are dependent upon are as much philosophical as practical, and, as such, demanded philosophical and not merely practical analysis.[19] Overall, however, despite these important differences, there are clear parallels between the two thinkers; Oakeshott and Winch share much in terms of their approaches to the relationship between rules, practices and self-conscious reflection.

The final way in which we will seek to contextualize Oakeshott's thought is by comparing it to that of the 'Cold War liberals'. Even to use this term is to court a certain amount of controversy, since precisely how 'Cold War liberalism' should be defined is a highly contested question, and hence, by extension, exactly which post-war thinkers count as 'Cold War liberals' is also controversial. (Indeed, for many, the very term 'Cold War liberal' remains a purely pejorative one, implying that a thinker is more committed to the cause of anti-totalitarian – and particularly anti-Soviet – ideology than they are to genuine philosophical inquiry.[20]) Nevertheless, at the risk of some simplification, it is possible to identify four key traits that such thinkers have in common, and we will use the prominent post-war thinkers Isaiah Berlin, Raymond Aron and Karl Popper to illustrate these.[21] First, in common with a number of other post-war political thinkers, they were unquestionably affected by the hegemony of positivism, which, as we have seen, contended in particular that statements of value could not be derived from statements of fact. It is true that this contention was supported by a number of different, discrete arguments, and some were certainly rejected by the Cold War liberals. Thus they had no time either for the argument that human conduct can be explained, potentially at least, entirely in causal terms, as A. J. Ayer claimed (see Ayer 1967) – hence proving normative claims either unnecessary or meaningless – or for the idea that the success of welfare state capitalism in the post-war period proved that the traditional problems of political theory had been – in practice at least – solved.[22] But they *were* to some extent affected by the pervasive post-war belief that, in view of the degree of moral and political pluralism exhibited by modern societies, it was difficult for political philosophers (or anyone else) to come up with genuinely normative arguments about politics and society. If Cold War liberals tended to be sceptical of the idea that scientific positivism such as Weldon's had proved that only verifiable (or analytic) statements were meaningful, they were nevertheless impressed by the more Weberian contention that values in modern societies were irretrievably divergent from one another.

Second, however, more positively, thinkers such as Berlin, Aron and Popper did not conclude from this that the degree of political pluralism found in modernity meant that political theory was impossible as a discipline. Still less did they argue, as such thinkers as Leo Strauss did, that modern pluralism was a symptom of a deeper malaise associated with modernity which should incline us to turn back to the eternal truths of classical political theory in general, and those of 'natural right' in particular (see Strauss 1953; Strauss 1959). Rather, they accepted the plural condition of modern man as a given, and rejected any attempt to explain human history by using a single artificial, theoretical construction, whether this was Strauss's conception of 'natural right', or, more commonly, some form of Marx's materialism[23] – albeit, admittedly, that they formulated their criticisms of Marxism in somewhat different ways. (Thus for Berlin, Marx's argument was reprehensible because it maintained that all of human history was determined, and, perhaps more deeply, because it implicitly claimed there was agreement about fundamental ethical and political concepts that did not exist.[24] By contrast for Aron, Marx's arguments in favour of a determined human history could be seen to be irrational because they remained tied to their original religious origins. And lastly, for Popper, what made Marx's position dubious was that it could not be formulated in such a manner that it could be tested and [potentially] falsified, the guarantee of all reputable theories – not least because it posited an unjustifiable a priori 'holism' about the nature of society that insulated its dictates from further criticism [Popper 1957: 66–9].) Instead, Cold War liberals argued that this should be taken as the point at which political theory should begin, and sometimes even that a plurality of values was the very precondition for political theory being possible at all. Thus for Berlin in particular it is precisely because meaningful normative questions about justice and liberty cannot be resolved empirically that makes political theory a viable discipline.[25]

Finally, following on from the second point, although they thought that drawing normative conclusions in an era of extensive pluralism was difficult, Cold War liberals thought that it was far from impossible. In particular, they argued that since values were largely incommensurable with one another, any position that claimed there was one correct, true path that all should follow was false, arguing on this basis that the individuality of different human beings in society should be respected. Part of their case for this position was a negative utilitarian one, most clearly exhibited in Popper's writings, namely that in the absence of one indubitable set of values, more pain was likely to be avoided by respecting and upholding the rights of individual citizens within a given society. But they also, more positively, tended to argue in favour of some version of the Kantian principle that other humans should not be used as ends[26] – ultimately because they believed that there was a reasonable chance that respecting individuality in this way would lead to the achievement of an harmonious and prosperous society, despite the deep conflict of values in modernity. (Thus Aron, for example, argued that since it was virtually impossible in practice to live in a situation where there were permanent warring values, arguing that one ultimately simply had to take a 'bet on humanity', while Berlin, when confronted with this problem, tended to refer vaguely to 'the human horizon' that all men and women share.) None of these thinkers offered a detailed set of institutional prescriptions to ensure that individual rights with a society would be respected – unlike F. A. Hayek, with whom they are often compared (see Hayek 1960; Hayek 1973–79). What they did do was to emphasize the importance of having a responsible and well-educated civil service, and a moderate and open political culture in doing this – in which, Aron stressed in particular, 'intellectuals' within society were not so purely 'oppositional' that they automatically declined to assist government in its tasks, and so abstractly critical that they were necessarily destructive of a nation's prevailing traditions.[27] Interestingly too, though the Cold War liberals in general declined to produce detailed institutional prescriptions for how the state should operate, none of the thinkers we are considering concluded from their stress on the importance of individuality that only minimal government intervention in economy and society should be allowed, again differing from the more doctrinaire free market arguments of Hayek. On the contrary, all thought that a critical part of enjoying individuality fully was a feeling of security, a security that could only come from knowing that a properly funded welfare state was on hand to pick up the pieces if all went awry. Thus despite being now widely associated with the New Right, Popper in fact remained on balance convinced of the virtues of the welfare state, Berlin continued to uphold the importance of positive as well as negative liberty – at least as a contending value – and Aron, despite some equivocations, remained convinced of the value of a welfare state to deal with the problems thrown up by the 'industrial society'.[28] And indeed, it was in fact Aron who most explicitly criticized Hayek's conception of liberty, precisely because he thought Hayek's dismissal of social justice was simply unhistorical, wilfully ignoring the needs of individuals in a modern society (Aron 1961; Aron 1969). But overall, however, although Cold War liberalism certainly did not lack the ability to mount normative arguments, it also had distinct weaknesses in its failure to justify fully its Kantian faith in humanity, and its lack of a closely argued position in favour of a particular set of institutions.

How does Oakeshott's thought compare to that of the Cold War liberals? There are three important similarities. First, as we have seen, although affected by positivism to the extent that he was at best tentative about seeking to justify normative political arguments by philosophical means, like the Cold War liberals Oakeshott denied this meant that the discipline of political philosophy was impossible, and in particular had no time for the idea that it was redundant because human conduct could be solely explained satisfactorily in causal terms. Moreover second, also like Berlin, Aron and Popper, as we have seen Oakeshott was keenly aware of the plural nature of modern life and chose to accept this plurality as a given, rather than seeking to impose one particular vision on modern society – whether this be the classic values of Leo Strauss or the pre-Renaissance ones advocated by Collingwood in his early work. This meant, finally, in the same way as these thinkers, Oakeshott sought to uphold the importance of individualism in modernity, strongly rejecting any account of the state that undermined this by imposing one particular normative end upon a disparate group of citizens. It is clear, therefore, that Oakeshott and the Cold War liberals not only share some important concerns, they also share some of the same normative arguments.

However, equally there are some significant differences, which mean that Oakeshott's work cannot simply be identified with that of the Cold War liberals, any more than Hayek's. Two in particular are especially significant. First, as we have seen, Oakeshott conceptualizes modernity in a different way from Berlin, Aron and Popper, viewing its irresolvable conflict of values far more unequivocally as a matter for celebration, rather than regret. Unlike the Cold War liberals, in other words, who tended to accept an essentially Weberian account of modernity whereby modern pluralism was achieved only at the cost of a radical break with tradition, as part of a radical 'disenchantment' with the world, for Oakeshott the situation is different. As far as he is concerned, a commitment to pluralist individualism is something that has been bequeathed to us as part of the Western tradition itself, so that it is unnecessary to support this by self-consciously applying individualist 'rules' or 'ideals' – whether they are based on either negative utilitarian or Kantian arguments. (Indeed, as we have seen, these are likely to be harmful, as far as Oakeshott is concerned, since they represent one-sided rationalist abstractions that are incapable of capturing all the complexities inherent in traditional experience.) Rather than modernity being seen as a brand new situation where we cannot look to our traditions to help us very much, in other words, as the Cold War liberals argue, for Oakeshott the situation is different: a commitment to individualism and pluralism is something we can derive from tradition. Second, in some ways following on from this, because Oakeshott sees the conflict of values we find in the modern world as bequeathed to us by tradition, rather than being unprecedented, he thinks more positively about how these values can be reconciled with one another, seeking in particular to find a political solution to deal with the problem. Unlike the Cold War liberals, who tended to maintain that values in modernity diverged from one another so starkly that it was difficult to find political institutions capable of respecting all the citizens' competing points of view, Oakeshott believes that it is possible to formulate a set of institutions that can respect individual freedom – indeed, like Hobbes, he believed that some kind of 'civil association' was necessary for citizens to be able to enjoy their individuality at all (see O'Sullivan 1999: 72; 79–84). So unlike the Cold War liberals, and particularly Berlin, Oakeshott had no time for the argument that laws could only ever reduce liberty, and constrain the options of individuals. Instead, he argued – in a ways that much more resemble Hayek or H. L. A. Hart – without the right kind of political institutions, and laws that were passed correctly, there could be no true freedom at all (see Hayek 1960; Hart 1961: chapter 2, section III, 2 above).

Overall, then, although assessing exactly what the 'reception' of Oakeshott's work was during his lifetime is difficult, since he tended to eschew the limelight and avoided direct confrontations with other influential thinkers, we have seen it is far from impossible. By comparing Oakeshott's work with that of other thinkers it is possible to understand better both the motivation behind his work and what makes his arguments distinctive. This is certainly so when examining *Experience and Its Modes* – which, as we saw, is better understood not merely as part of Oakeshott's attempt to analyse the relationship between philosophy and other modes of understanding, but also, more specifically, as a response to R. G. Collingwood's critique of the nature of modernity in *Speculum Mentis*. But it is perhaps even more true of Oakeshott's post-war work, where, again as we saw, a comparison of Oakeshott's work with that of Weldon, Winch and the Cold War liberals reveals that his arguments have much in common with those of his contemporaries – whilst at the same time being fascinatingly different from them. Thus although Oakeshott agreed with Weldon – ostensibly at least – that philosophizing was little use in practice, he nevertheless disagreed sharply with him over the verification principle and over the primacy of science as an explanatory language more generally. And equally, while Oakeshott certainly concurred with Winch over the impossibility of explaining human conduct causally, instead seeing it as shaped by rules and practices, he nevertheless disagreed with him on the relationship between thought and language and that between philosophy and practice. And finally, while Oakeshott shares much with the Cold War liberals, not least in his strong support for pluralism against any attempt to impose one particular vision on modern society, he also importantly differed from them in seeking to find a means of reconciling different individual interests institutionally, through a particular kind of modern state. Although there are distinct similarities between Oakeshott's arguments and that of other thinkers, especially post-war ones, his position nevertheless remains very much his own.

Chapter 4

Oakeshott's Continuing Relevance: Some Meditations on Conservatism and Liberalism

As we have seen in previous chapters, although Oakeshott's work is written in a rather complicated style, it is genuinely rich in insights and covers a very wide variety of topics. As such, his work, elusive though it is, has been linked to a number of very different debates. Some of these have been mentioned already, including his contributions to the nature of aesthetics, to scientific method and to the philosophy of history. (Thus, as we have seen, he advocates a highly contemplative approach when dealing with artworks, a demandingly positivist position when it comes to science and strongly argues that historians should aim to construct a particular account of the past in response to an historical question – rather than aiming to capture the intentions of past actors or provide a fully objective account of the past [See above, chapter 2].) But Oakeshott's work has also been influential in a number of other spheres, especially in interpreting the work of Thomas Hobbes, in influencing how the discipline of politics is taught and in the philosophy of education. Thus Oakeshott advocates a particular reading of Hobbes's *Leviathan* (at least in his revised introduction) that insists Hobbes intended laws to be non-instrumental in nature, rejecting utilitarian justifications for the social contract (see especially Tregenza 2003: chapter 3) as well as advocating the study of the history of political thought as vital for the study of politics (see Kelly 1999; Kenny 2004), and more widely an approach to university education that stresses the importance of theoretical activities, of a 'holiday' from practical drudgery (Oakeshott 1991: 184–218; Podoksik 2003: 211–32). However, there are perhaps two debates in particular where Oakeshott's contributions are of particular importance, and which are of especial interest to political philosophers – although paradoxically they are also ones where he himself was not particularly explicit about his position. Thus, first, Oakeshott's political theory is of particular interest to those seeking to determine the precise nature of modern liberal and conservative ideologies – since there has been a considerable discussion about how the boundary between the two should be defined, and Oakeshott appears to exhibit key features of both.[1] And second, as has been indicated in previous chapters, one of the key features of Oakeshott's thought is that it offers (implicitly at least) a distinctive view of the nature of modernity – a question that has exercised a wide variety of contemporary theorists, including Arendt, Gadamer, Foucault and Habermas, to name only the most famous. For reasons of space, we will only investigate the first of these debates here – although there is certainly scope for scholars to make sustained comparisons between Oakeshott and the other thinkers on the nature of tradition, the Enlightenment, modernity, individuality and their differing interpretations of Aristotle (see Dallmayr 1984; Canovan 1997 for some initial comparisons).

Turning to the debate about ideologies, then, to assess why it is difficult to determine what the boundary between liberalism and conservatism is, and to determine how to locate Oakeshott ideologically, it obviously follows that a definition of both 'liberalism' and 'conservatism' must be attempted. Doing so is obviously a far from easy task, however, even if we limit ourselves to Western Europe since not only are both the nature of liberalism and conservatism strongly contested, but have also significantly altered their meaning over time.[2] Hence not merely a synchronic, but also a diachronic analysis of ideology is necessary if we are going to locate a political theorist correctly. Thus, if we take liberalism first, it seems relatively uncontroversial to claim that, despite some important precursors, the ideology arose due to significant new demands for individual freedom in the late eighteenth century, partly due to important philosophical innovations connected with the Enlightenment, and partly stimulated by significant social and political changes that took their most dramatic form in the French Revolution. And more specifically, it seems reasonable to claim that liberals have tended to advocate five fundamental normative goals to increase such freedom. First, they have tended to favour greater political liberty, on the basis that mankind in general has a broadly equal potential to reason, rather than being naturally hierarchical. Second, they have also tended to stress the beneficial effects that the free use of this reason would lead to, arguing that greater liberty would lead to greater progress. Third, this claim about progress has often (if not exclusively) been linked to the contention that only government by a nation-state could ensure prosperity and freedom, thus providing liberals with a specific normative goal in the political sphere. Fourthly, liberals have tended to stress the importance of individuals having economic freedom, instead of labouring under 'artificial' constraints of governmental regulation and monopolies, on the basis that would aid the prosperity of the society as a whole, while finally they have also tended to have great respect for property rights and property laws, since these are not only necessary to maintain basic order and security within a given state, but also to ensure that individuals are able to have the means to express their personalities on a concrete basis within the state.

However, although it is reasonable to suggest that liberals have broadly shared a commitment to these arguments, this is not to suggest that they have given each of them equal weight, even in the nineteenth century, let alone subsequently. Thus even the first liberals split into at least three distinct groups. First, one set took it as all but self-evident that the best way to safeguard individual liberty was to limit interference from others, but especially from the state, arguing that individuals should have the maximum liberty possible in both economic and political spheres. It is true that though this group differed as to precisely why they favoured this position – with utilitarians (such as Jeremy Bentham) favouring greater liberty because it maximized human pleasure, while more romantic thinkers (such as Wilhelm von Humboldt and John Stuart Mill) favouring it because it was the only way for individuals to develop their personalities fully, both morally and aesthetically – there was nevertheless no doubting the main thrust of their arguments (Bentham 1983: 196; Humboldt 1969: 108). Second, however, other liberals – such as Benjamin Constant and Alexis de Tocqueville – were far less convinced that simply increasing rights against state intervention was sufficient to guarantee genuine liberty. This was because they stressed that the rise of a more commercial society, and the resultant destruction of traditional local political and economic institutions would mean that the state's powers would necessarily grow (Tocqueville 1861). Because there would no longer be other bodies to which citizens could appeal to uphold their rights in modernity, such thinkers believed citizens would almost inevitably turn to the state, so that the only real way of securing individual liberty was to limit the power of the state more fundamentally by adopting some form of federalism. Finally, other liberals, such as G. W. F. Hegel and the British Whigs, argued that although it was important for individuals to have certain rights against government intervention, it was nevertheless only in the context of the nation-state that they could gain true liberty. To some extent they resembled Constant and de Tocqueville, in that they rejected the contention that liberty could be gained just by ensuring that individuals had freedom from constraint to pursue their own life-plans. But they also differed importantly from these French thinkers by arguing far less ambivalently that the nation-state represented an improvement on previous governmental arrangements, and was, moreover, itself an important motor for liberal progress – part of which, particularly in Hegel's case, consisted in the achievement of a more laudable character-type (Hegel 1952: 160–1).

Though all these nineteenth century thinkers certainly favoured the augmentation of personal liberty, they nevertheless still disagreed significantly amongst themselves as to what this implied in practice. And if anything, such disagreements over the nature of liberalism subsequently increased, in response in particular to the industrialization and urbanization of the nineteenth century, the twentieth century experience of two world wars and the considerably greater moral pluralism. This in turn led to the development of four further types of liberalism, which, although still firmly related to earlier kinds, were nevertheless importantly distinct. First, in response to an increasingly industrialized society, such New Liberal thinkers as L. T. Hobhouse and J. A. Hobson responded by arguing that the liberals' traditional suspicion of state intervention in the economy should be revised, since socio-economic pressures posed much more of a threat to liberty than had been previously argued. And in view of this, they argued, the state should provide a far greater level of public services (including state-maintained libraries and museums, and support for hospitals and public transport), as well as – more fundamentally – intervening in the economy in order to ensure an individual's right to work, since otherwise they would not be truly free (Hobhouse 1911: 163). Although such thinkers continued to uphold some of the most important core liberal tenets, including the value of personal liberty and the importance of free trade, they nevertheless posited a far greater role for the state. Second, however, less positively, other liberals (most notably Max Weber) suggested that such socio-economic difficulties could not be solved simply by increasing state intervention, since they were not simply temporary problems but were rather intrinsic to the very nature of modernity. To some extent Weber was simply restating the worries of such earlier thinkers as Constant and de Tocqueville in saying this, warning of the dislocating effects of a more industrialized society – but he went beyond them in arguing that not merely were there resolvable *tensions* in modernity, but that these were the product of 'irreducibly competing ideals'. As such, Weber was sceptical of the New Liberals' position that one could easily use state intervention to increase the freedom of individuals in society – since their moral perspectives were far too diverse to accomplish this with much certainty, and in any case all modern organizations (the state included) had a tendency to bureaucratic atrophy. So although Weber remained recognizably liberal – in that he continued to support such classic liberal objectives as increasing the electoral franchise, upholding the rule of law and increasing the rights of parliament against the executive and rejecting a return to premodern traditions – this was as much an attempt to stave off bureaucracy and cope with a unprecedented degree of pluralism, as it was an optimistic attempt to increase the freedom of all (Weber 1994: 222).

Increasingly, the challenge that such pluralism posed proved to be the conundrum that later twentieth-century liberals found most pressing. To deal with it, they essentially mounted two (very different) responses. One was essentially a libertarian response, which was put forward by thinkers like Hayek and the 'Cold War liberals' we examined in the last chapter. These thinkers accepted Weber's contention that in modernity it would never be possible to reconcile different values with one another through the use of reason, and, as such, argued that the best that one could do was to ensure that citizens had the maximum amount of individual liberty to pursue their own ends, at best backing this up with badly supported Kantian intuitions in favour of individual dignity (see Chapter 3, above). More recently, however, other thinkers have sought to overcome the moral pluralism associated with modernity far more ambitiously, using various philosophical devices to try and derive a normative commitment to prioritize the value of individual liberty – not as a 'least worst' option, but rather as positive good (Rawls 1971: 5). Obviously the most famous thinker to do this was John Rawls, who argued in his early work that by inviting human beings to imagine themselves behind a 'veil of ignorance', before they knew their position in society, one could deduce that they would favour both individual liberty and an important measure of equality – so that only inequalities that maximized the overall well-being of all would be countenanced. Rival thinkers, by contrast (such as Joseph Raz), argued that such a commitment to individual liberty could only be favoured if one actively favoured a particular character-type within society, rather than claiming one could be purely neutral, as Rawls had (Raz 1986: 369), while others again have contended that a much stronger commitment to equality is necessary for individuals to be genuinely free. In all cases, however, such 'philosophical liberals', as they have been dubbed, are committed to finding some universalist position, however modest, that is able to conquer the problem of modern pluralism. For them, albeit more modestly than in the nineteenth century, reason retains its power to support a commitment to individual liberty.

If liberalism, despite all its variations, has always represented a relatively coherent ideology (namely one that has sought to prioritize promoting individual liberty as a normative goal), by contrast conservatism has always been a much looser construction that has included a wider range of positions within it – especially after the middle of the nineteenth century. Arising in reaction to the social and political changes that had taken place in the eighteenth century, exemplified most dramatically by the French Revolution, conservatives initially took aim at a variety of Enlightenment assumptions – including, variously, its claim that all men had more or less equal powers of reasoning, its scepticism about religious belief and its demands for greater political and economic freedom from the state. Whilst is true that virtually no early nineteenth century conservative thought it was feasible to dispense with the whole of the Enlightenment heritage *tout court* (either intellectually or in practice) and even the most reactionary conservative accepted that a return to the *ancien regime* was impossible, they nevertheless rejected enough to stake out a position that was distinctively different from liberalism. Thus, for example, Edmund Burke, the first real conservative theorist, emphasized the extent to which societies were composed organically and were reliant on tradition so that any attempt to redesign them consciously was likely to fail; he argued that modern commercial freedoms were dependent on pre-modern traditions, rather than being independent, as liberals argued (Burke 1826: 155). And more radically Joseph de Maistre, although he grudgingly advocated coming to terms with the new representative institutions in France, vehemently rejected the idea that citizens should obey the state because it was the best way of securing freedom, arguing instead that their obligation to do so was based upon a religious and emotional bond, and not just upon instrumental calculation. For both, the pursuit of individual freedom was to be rejected (or at least subordinated) in favour of other goals – namely, promoting religious belief; traditional, social and political hierarchies or more generally the nation-state in general, which it was essential (they believed) to conceptualize in organic rather than individualistic terms.

This, then, was the initial form that conservatism took. Like liberalism, however, although it did not alter completely in response to industrialization and greater pluralism, it was nevertheless forced to adapt in response to these pressures. Some conservative thinkers reacted very radically, taking such developments as a sign that not merely should that reject liberal arguments, but modernity as a whole. Thus, to give two very different examples, Thomas Carlyle argued romantically against industrialization and representative government, instead seeking – in such works as *Heroes and*

Hero-worship and the *Latter-Day Pamphlets* – to uphold the virtues of religion and heroic despotism, while Friedrich Nietzsche went even further, criticizing not merely modern social and political arrangements, but also the Western tradition itself for its adherence to ascetic Christian norms or charity and forgiveness, arguing that such norms had inevitably weakened mankind's ability to express its potentially heroic nature (Nietzsche 1994: 29). In general, however, the reactions were more moderate, and centred on upholding two commitments in particular. In the first place, conservatives continued to stress that the nation-state had conceptual priority over the individual, arguing that this should be the fundamental unit to which citizens should have allegiance, both nationally and internationally. At the end of the nineteenth century such arguments were supported by the intellectual popularity of social Darwinism – in the work of Benjamin Kidd and Heinrich von Treitschke – since this could provide a reason why nations might compete; but even after World War II, when social Darwinism had lost popularity, conservatives continued to uphold the importance of the nation-state, though latterly they often combined this with an increasing willingness to intervene in the economy to maintain social solidarity. Secondly, however, other conservatives sought to colonize territory vacated by liberal thinkers, upholding the importance of freedom from the state, defending commerce from government intervention and (more often than not) advocating laissez-faire. Thus a number of former liberal thinkers such as Herbert Spencer became increasingly difficult to distinguish from conservatives like Lord Hugh Cecil by the end of the nineteenth century – despite some residual differences over issues like imperialism and franchise reform (Spencer 1909: 87) – and this type of conservatism was to be re-energized again by the reaction to a more interventionist state after World War II, and the perceived failure of Keynesian economics in the 1970s. Distinguishing between types of conservatism in this way, of course, is not to suggest that there were no attempts at combining them: Margaret Thatcher's attempt to combine a strong commitment to nationalism with an equally strong commitment to a free market represents only one such attempt.

As this sketch reveals, therefore, determining precisely what makes a 'conservative' and what makes a 'liberal' is far from simple, since despite having attained a certain amount of coherence, each ideological family also contains within it a host of different potential positions. Furthermore, it is not possible to identify the ideological affiliation of a political thinker by observing that he or she espouses one particular political value, since a particular normative end – such as, for example upholding the importance of 'private property' – can form an important part of more than one ideology. (Thus in this case, for example, although conservatives have had periods of espousing protectionism and liberals of advocating state intervention in the economy, both have tended to be supporters of the free market, more often than not.) Rather, the critical point as Michael Freeden has notably demonstrated, is how 'core' a particular component is, and what its relationship to the other components within the ideology is – so that arguably a liberal must be concerned with increasing individual liberty as an overriding priority, whatever other ends he or she also espouses (Freeden 1996: 84). By contrast a conservative, though he or she may also treat advocating freedom as an important end will arguably subordinate this, ultimately at least, to other goals such as tradition or the nation-state. Nevertheless, despite this insight, determining in practice where the boundary between 'liberalism' and 'conservatism' should fall is still controversial, partly because (as we have seen) determining what individual liberty actually means remains controversial, but partly simply because determining which concepts an individual thinker is prioritizing in any case can be far from easy. How then should we place Oakeshott, and what does his work tell us about the two ideologies we are considering?

At first sight, the strong implication of the argument of the two previous chapters might seem to be to categorize Oakeshott as a liberal, since clearly a commitment to individual freedom is something that he prizes very highly. Clearly, Oakeshott cannot be identified as a liberal like Rawls, since he does not believe that the problem of modern pluralism can be overcome philosophically, on a universal moral basis. (Because Oakeshott does not believe that moral practices can be self-consciously harmonized with one another, in other words, it would be fruitless to try and establish any kind of philosophical consensus on the moral ends of the state.) But there seems to be a much stronger argument to suggest that Oakeshott can be plausibly identified as a libertarian liberal who to some extent resembles Hayek – in other words someone who accepts that moral pluralism cannot be overcome philosophically, and therefore tries to formulate governmental institutions to maximize individual liberty – and for this reason a number of commentators have attempted to interpret Oakeshott's work in this way. One obvious difficulty with this view is that unlike Hayek and many libertarians, Oakeshott specifically rejects the view that the purpose of the state is to maximize economic productivity, since, as we have seen, he is emphatic that a 'civil association' should not have any substantive end. (Hence one of liberalism's traditional reasons for advocating increased political liberty is rejected.) But commentators on Oakeshott, such as Paul Franco, have argued that this is in fact a strength, not a weakness, and confirms Oakeshott's status as a liberal thinker, since what he is actually doing is 'purging' the liberal tradition of a foreign element, hence bestowing a new coherence upon the liberal tradition (Franco 1990b: 9, 159–60, 231). Rather than muddling up liberalism with the aim of economic productivity, or pursuing socio-economic equality (like the New Liberals), or the possibility of progress (like most nineteenth century liberals), according to Franco, what Oakeshott does is to concentrate on the core of liberalism, at least as it has evolved in the twentieth century: accepting that individuals are genuinely different from one other, providing a state with laws that cater for this and mechanisms for upholding individuals' private property and the free market so that they can express their individuality properly.[3] Furthermore, as other commentators on Oakeshott, such as Efraim Podoksik, have stressed, although there is no general belief in 'progress' *per se* (as was common amongst nineteenth-century liberals), unlike Hayek and the Cold War liberals, Oakeshott certainly anticipated that citizens might take considerable *enjoyment* from their individuality – at least if they were capable of adjusting to modernity properly (see e.g. Podoksik 2003: 166–8).[4] For Podoksik, this 'anarchic', 'existentialist' aspect of Oakeshott's thought is better seen as evidence of a 'romantic liberal' side to his position – so that, although part of his justification for 'civil association' is (like Hayek's) based upon epistemological scepticism, equally it is also based upon the demand by individuals for a state in which they can truly express themselves. If there is no room for Mill's argument that a wide latitude for eccentricity is necessary for social development, such eccentricity (so the argument runs) is still valuable in itself: only in such a way can the plurality of individual experience be respected.

However, there are several problems with this argument, which suggest that Oakeshott's position is, on balance, better described as 'conservative', rather than 'liberal'. Certainly, as we saw, it is difficult to describe him as a 'conservative' in the sense of someone who thoroughly rejects the Enlightenment as a whole, since – except in a few of his middle-period essays, such as 'Rationalism in Politics' – Oakeshott is a firm supporter of modernity, both philosophically and in practice. And furthermore, despite a brief flirtation with rejecting the Western tradition as a whole in 'The Tower of Babel', still less can Oakeshott be identified as a 'conservative' like Nietzsche or Leo Strauss, since usually he is adamant that upholding the best parts of our tradition is a vital part of 'disclosing' and 'enacting' ourselves successfully, to use the terminology of *On Human Conduct*. But as the delineation of conservative ideology given earlier suggests, this does not imply that one must accept that Oakeshott is actually a liberal, since most forms of European conservatism have in fact been modernist, and, moreover, have been highly adept at absorbing parts of liberal ideology that the liberals have vacated. What, then, marks out Oakeshott's position as conservative rather than liberal?

Essentially, there are two reasons. In the first place, although he is rarely explicit about it, there is a much stronger sense in Oakeshott's work than one would expect from a late twentieth-century liberal of the value of the nation-state, and beyond this of the importance of patriotism in general. If 'tradition' is something that Oakeshott is concerned to value, by this he means – primarily at least – a national tradition, rather than something more international. This strongly contrasts with most recent thinkers in the liberal tradition, including Hayek – who was a strong supporter of some form of European union, and opposed to nationalism – and most of the Cold War liberals, due to the experiences of World War II, though Berlin was something of an exception. (Even here, arguably Berlin was concerned to point out that nationalism was a phenomenon that was unavoidable, rather than that it was something positively desirable.) And second, related to this, although just like a liberal thinker Oakeshott constantly upholds the value of individuality, and on this basis advocates the importance of individual liberty, ultimately (as we noted in the last chapter), this is something that he does on the basis that it is an important value that has been bequeathed to us by tradition. Rather than claiming that liberty should be valued because we have a fundamental right to it as human beings, or because it enables us to develop our abilities to the full, as we have seen for Oakeshott its value ultimately remains related to the tradition into which we have been socialized. Although Podoksik is undoubtedly right to suggest that Oakeshott intends us to enjoy the individualism that has fortunately developed in modernity, therefore, ultimately this is something that must be put down to good fortune – unlike most liberal thinkers, Oakeshott has no rational justification for the individualism that has appeared in modernity, just as he has no justification for the fortunate development of a sophisticated plurality of non-philosophical theoretical disciplines that enable us to understand the world fruitfully. And whilst it could be objected that this is equally true of libertarian thinkers like Hayek – since they also tend to stress that the spontaneous order which guarantees liberty in modernity cannot be fully understood by our powers of reason, so that rational planning is impossible – arguably there is also a crucial difference. For although libertarians agree with conservatives that the complexity of modern society means that reason lacks the power to plan for future events successfully, they nevertheless often add further justifications in favour of liberty that go beyond merely looking to tradition. In particular libertarians like Hayek and Robert Nozick specifically argue that the only constraint that a state is justified in trying to remove when it comes to upholding a citizen's liberty is one that is *intentionally designed* – so that, for example, a citizen should be protected against the activities of thieves, but not against those of extreme imbalances in the market (Hayek 1978: 19). By contrast, a true conservative will not – ultimately at least – accept justifications for individual liberty that go beyond those that have been bequeathed us by tradition. And by this definition Oakeshott is a conservative, not a libertarian. To 'purge' liberalism, in short, as Franco suggests Oakeshott does, therefore, may well be to lead to a relatively coherent political position. But the outcome is not a liberal position. It is a moderate conservative one.

Notes

Chapter 2

1. For the famous comment that 'for the moment, anyway, political philosophy is dead', see Laslett (1956: vii).
2. Others include Patrick Gardiner, Arthur Danto and W. B. Gallie (Gardiner 1952; Danto 1965; Gallie 1964).
3. The idea that 'falsifiability' – rather than verifiability – constitutes the criterion for what is a genuinely scientific (or social scientific) hypothesis was propagated by Karl Popper (Popper 1957).
4. For classic texts in the modern hermeneutic and pragmatic traditions, see Gadamer (1989) and Rorty (1980); for an attempt to locate Oakeshott's position in these developments, see Dallmayr (1984).
5. Rawls developed his conception of an 'overlapping consensus' in Rawls (1995) and subsequent works, as a response to the criticism that in Rawls (1971) he had yoked his definition of justice too closely to an advocacy of a particular (Kantian) conception of autonomy. By contrast, the idea of an 'overlapping consensus' conjectures that reasonable citizens within a well-ordered society can still agree on a political conception of justice, whilst differing sharply over their comprehensive moral worldviews. So although a reasonable Kantian and a reasonable utilitarian might be diametrically opposed over how to judge actions morally, they can still advocate the same political conception of justice – the Kantian because it best promotes individual autonomy; the utilitarian because it best promotes overall utility. See Rawls (1999: 42) 'political liberalism does not . . . try to fix public reason once and for all in the form of one favoured conception of justice'. Critics have argued, however,

that notwithstanding Rawls's claims to neutrality, he is still committed to a substantive conception of what being 'reasonable' consists of here.

6. The phrase was originally Bernard Bosanquet's, see Bosanquet (1923: 2).

7. Podoksik and Tseng differ sharply over both of these issues – though it should be noted that it is quite possible to maintain (as I do) that Oakeshott is a defender of modernity (pace Tseng), but nevertheless a particular kind of conservative, not a liberal (pace Podoksik) (see chapter 4). In general, however, Podoksik's reading of Oakeshott is much more convincing; for some criticisms of Tseng's reading, see Neill (2004).

8. Nardin is the clearest (and most persuasive) advocate of reading Oakeshott as a pure philosopher; for a much more 'political' approach, see John Gray's reading of Oakeshott's work, in, for example, Gray (1993: 40–6).

9. To Podoksik, I am indebted not merely for his insistence that Oakeshott is best read as a modernist overall, but also for his more specific argument that what is most significant about *Experience and Its Modes* is Oakeshott's depiction of specific modes, not his alleged continuing commitment to Absolute Idealism – see Podoksik (2003). My interpretation of Oakeshott's work has also been influenced by the work of Paul Franco and Terry Nardin – see Franco (1990b), Franco (2004), and Nardin (2001).

10. For a very helpful account of Oakeshott's relationship with British Idealist philosophy, by which I have been particularly influenced, see Franco (2004), chapter 2. Also very useful on British Idealism and Idealism more generally are Quinton (1971) and Hylton (1990).

11. As Harold Joachim puts it, for example: 'what is immediately experienced perplexes us and sets us thinking; but the moment we begin to think, we are transforming [it] ... Often, no doubt, the mediation is but the bringing out what the initial Immediacy really is ... But neither the process itself nor its result ... – neither reasoning nor the reasoned understanding to which it leads – ... are logical consequents or logical grounds of the initial Immediacy'. See Joachim (1919: 11).

12. To quote F. H. Bradley, for example: 'my object is to have a world as comprehensive and coherent as possible ... [so that]

facts ... are true ... just so far as they work, just so far as they contribute to the order of experience.' This means, he argues, 'if by taking certain judgements of perception as true, I can get more system into my world, then these "facts" are so far true, and if by taking certain "facts" as errors I can order my experience better, then so far these "facts" are errors'. See Bradley (1914: 210).

13 As Bernard Bosanquet puts it, for example: 'the endeavour of the simple generalisation is to pursue an identity apart from differences. Its method, therefore, is omission. The generality is formed by attending to the common qualities of a number of individuals, and disregarding their differences.' See Bosanquet (1912b: 34–5).

14 To quote Bosanquet again: 'we all of us experience the Absolute, because the Absolute is in everything. And as it is in everything we do or suffer, we may even say that we experience it more fully than we experience anything else, especially as one profound characterisation runs through the whole. And that is, that the world does not let us alone'. See Bosanquet (1912a: 27).

15 See Bradley (1968: 319–20) where he insists that all our judgments provided by thought imply something beyond it. (As he puts it: 'all our judgments, to be true, must become conditional. The predicate, that is, does not hold unless by the help of something else. And this "something else" cannot be stated'.) By contrast the Absolute (or 'Reality') appears to us without any such mediation, and it cannot directly be inferred from our principles, or indeed from any other results of thought. For although 'our principles may by true ... they are not reality. They no more *make* that Whole which commands our devotion, than some shredded dissection of human tatters *is* that warm and breathing beauty of flesh which our hearts found delightful'. See Bradley (1922: 50).

16 The best the state can do, according to Bosanquet is to ensure it 'forcibly hinders a hindrance to the best life or common good'; it cannot promote that common good directly. See Bosanquet (1923: 178 and more widely, chapter 8, 167–217).

17 As Collingwood puts it, commenting on how 'history' exposes his previous modes as being inadequate: 'all art, religion, and science rest on ... history, as the earlier terms of any

dialectical series [depend] on the later ... The terms of a dialectical series are not related to one another in terms of degree, but by the assertion in each ... of something which in the previous [mode] ... was wrongly denied' (Collingwood 1924: 207–8).

[18] In contrast with the modes, where there is necessarily an 'element of necessary and insurmountable error', Collingwood argues, 'in the life of philosophy ... the mind ... says what is means, and therefore can for the first time say what is absolutely true' (Collingwood 1924: 295).

[19] For Bradley, 'it is only a view which asserts degrees of reality and truth, and which has a rational meaning for words such as "higher" or "lower" – it is only such a view which can do justice to the sides of idea and existence' (Bradley 1968: 354).

[20] Oakeshott does not definitively rule out such concepts being reformulated quantitatively in *Experience and Its Modes* – but neither does he make any suggestion as to how one would do so.

[21] Cf. especially Oakeshott (1933: 291): 'Practice is the alteration of one given world of ideas so as to make it agree with another given world of ideas, and this alteration is, in fact, the making coherent of the world of practical experience.'

[22] As Collingwood explains: the artist's business 'is to speak out ... But what he has to utter is not ... his own secret ... The reason why they need him is that no community altogether knows its own heart; and by failing in this knowledge a community deceives itself on the one subject concerning which ignorance means death ... Art is the community's medicine for the worst disease of the mind, the corruption of consciousness'. See Collingwood (1938: 336).

[23] The implication seems to be that even in identifying a particular disease, it is not enough to have a checklist of symptoms; rather, one *must* also have practical experience of treating the disease in question.

[24] Bacon remains highly suspect, however, as far as Oakeshott is concerned, and remains so throughout his career. See Oakeshott (1975: 287–91).

[25] Arguably it is possible to see how the kind of technical knowledge that consists of purely formal rules could be formulated

entirely independently of any practical ability, but much harder to see how technical knowledge that is supposed to help perform an activity successfully could be formulated in this way. Thus drawing up the rules for a game (such as chess) might be done independently of playing the game – though even here one suspects they will often be amended as a result of playing the game in practice – but it is much harder to see how rules designed to help one play the game well could be produced entirely independently from the practice of playing. Although Oakeshott does not explicitly make this distinction in *Rationalism in Politics*, the point still seems a reasonable one to make, since he cites both kinds of rules as examples of technical knowledge.

26 By extension the freedom of an Englishman cannot be defined as the implementation of a priori values; instead it must be seen as 'nothing more than arrangements, procedures of a certain kind; [so that] the freedom of an Englishman is not something exemplified in habeas corpus, it is, at that point, the availability of that procedure' (Oakeshott 1991: 121).

27 The prevalence of this interpretation can be shown by the degree to which even commentators who identify Oakeshott's political thought as 'liberal' nevertheless insist that he believes the post-Enlightenment Western political tradition to be suspect (see (Gray 1993: 40–6), for one example only.).

28 Oakeshott's language (and indeed argument) clearly derives from Hobbes here. Oakeshott's lifelong respect for Hobbes can easily be appreciated by examining Oakeshott (2000), which contains his famous 1948 'Introduction' to *Leviathan*.

29 Cf. also Oakeshott (1975: 6): 'A symbol is not an "object" in advance of being recognized as a symbol, and a picture does not need to be recognized as "paint on canvas" before it is understood or misunderstood as a "work of art"'.

30 Oakeshott makes his point here by pointedly contrasting his position with that of Plato in *The Republic*. For him knowledge of the sun proves no substitute for the knowledge of the cave. See Oakeshott (1975: 27–31).

31 The distinction between 'doing' and 'understanding' had to some extent been anticipated by the distinction between 'work' and 'play' that Oakeshott had written about in an

eponymous article, though he did not publish it in his lifetime. It is now available in Oakeshott (2004: 303–14).

32 The best psychologists and sociologists can do, Oakeshott maintains, following his position in *Experience and Its Modes*, is to identify surface regularities in human behaviour – the crucial point being that such an analysis does not confuse orders of inquiry.

33 This obviously implies that emotional responses qualify just as much as highly self-conscious ones (cf. Oakeshott 1975: 40). This contrasts with classifications of action – such as Max Weber's – that attempt to distinguish between *how* intelligent given responses are. More precisely, Weber claims that actions can be classified as belonging to one of four types. On a descending scale of rationality, these are, respectively: 'purposively rational' conduct, where there is both a clear end and a clear calculation as to the best means to obtain this end; 'value rational' action, where there is an overriding ideal rather than a clear end, but which nevertheless involves the setting of coherent objectives (for example, in the pursuit of 'duty') and 'affective' action, which is carried out under an emotional impulse and 'traditional' action, which is carried out under the influence of custom and habit. It should be stressed that Weber regards these depictions as 'ideal types', rather than types of behaviour that are often found in pure form; in practice, Weber believes, most actions will consist of at least two of these types. For these distinctions, cf. Weber (1968: i. 24–6).

34 For a related distinction concerning the differences between demonstrative and persuasive argument, cf. Oakeshott (1975: 49 n. 1).

35 In many ways this position echoes that of *Experience and Its Modes*, namely that because all practical judgment involves thought, it cannot be purely subjective.

36 As Oakeshott also puts it, they are to be seen as 'more durable relationships between agents which are not themselves transactions but are the conditional contexts of all such transactions' (Oakeshott 1975: 54).

37 This is simply stipulated without further argument by Oakeshott, and at first glance seems reasonable. But in fact it raises difficult questions for Oakeshott about the nature of power

in society, and, more widely, how he seeks to conceptualize it. For if by 'force', Oakeshott means literally physical force – as one might expect from a thinker so profoundly influenced by Hobbes – then this seems a relatively straightforward position, but one that ignores the obvious power imbalances that unquestionably (and intrinsically) exist within some practices. Is a practice where the *threat* of physical force is intrinsic to it, still a genuine practice as far as Oakeshott is concerned, for example? Conversely, if 'force' *does* include the phenomenon of the threat of force, then this raises the question of how *much* of an imbalance there must be for a practice to be illegitimate. Arguably neither of the two main influences on Oakeshott's position here – namely Hobbes, on the one hand, and the ordinary language philosophers like Ryle, on the other – are much use in helping Oakeshott to resolve this question, since their own conceptualizations of power are not particularly developed.

38 See the summary of this point by Hans-Georg Gadamer, another theorist profoundly affected by Aristotle, in Gadamer (1989: 321, n. 259).

39 As Gadamer puts it: 'the self-knowledge of which Aristotle speaks is characterized by the fact that it includes perfect application and employs its knowledge in the immediacy of the given situation'. See Gadamer (1989: 322).

40 As he puts it pointedly at Oakeshott (1975: 89), although the skill he is seeking to describe is 'akin to the Aristotelian *phronesis*', the difference is that 'whereas the aesthesis of the *phronimos* was, primarily, his understanding of how to act rightly . . . I am concerned with the understanding implicit both in acting and in acting rightly'.

41 Oakeshott is very clear that sentiments cannot be defined in terms of an agent's antecedent drives or tendency to choose particular actions. See Oakeshott (1975: 71).

42 It should be pointed out that this cultivation is far from inevitable. Oakeshott readily admits that not only can sentiments be mixed, but also that an agent can be acting in a particular sentiment and yet be quite unaware of doing so.

43 It is notable that Oakeshott only considers these two alternatives. Partly this can be explained, as indicated, by his strong

advocacy of the importance of plurality (and hence of a state to uphold this), but it is difficult to avoid the suspicion that Oakeshott sets the dichotomy up as a polemical contrast. If one rejects the idea that the state must pursue one substantive end in common, he seems to be arguing, then the only alternative is to uphold 'civil association'. This is not obviously true. Oakeshott's inspiration for this dichotomy ultimately comes from Otto von Gierke – see O'Sullivan (2000: 135–6).

44 Pursuing a common goal together is bad enough, according to Oakeshott, but aiming at perfection is certainly infinitely worse. For a slightly whimsical (if entertaining) view of what he sees as the consequences, see Michael Oakeshott's essay called 'The Tower of Babel' – at Oakeshott (1983: 179–210) – an essay which shares only its title with the one published in *Rationalism in Politics.*

45 On this basis, Oakeshott also famously denies that Hobbes's state has a substantive end. For the best analysis of Oakeshott's interpretation of Hobbes on this point, see Tregenza (2003), especially chapter 3.

46 Oakeshott's position strongly resembles that of Herbert Hart here: see Hart (1961), chapters 2–4.

47 As he puts it: 'The recognition of *respublica* [i.e. the comprehensive conditions of association] which constitutes civil association is neither approval of the conditions it prescribes nor expectations about the enforcement of these conditions; it is recognizing it as a system of law'. See Oakeshott (1975: 149).

48 The idea that one can do so is most commonly associated with Hans Kelsen. See, in particular, Kelsen (1989).

49 Moreover, though rarely accepted entirely, Oakeshott's account of history has attracted considerable attention and praise – not least from his distinguished fellow philosopher of history Collingwood, who called the section on history in *Experience and Its Modes* 'the most penetrating analysis of historical thought that has ever been written, and will remain a classic in that hitherto almost unexplored branch of philosophical research' (cf. Collingwood 1934: 249–50).

50 As one would expect, therefore, Oakeshott specifically denies Heidegger's contention that practical understanding is so 'primordial' that it can never be transcended by theoretical

inquiry – although it is notable that he concedes (with qualifications) that 'practical understanding . . . precedes any other mode of understanding in the life of a human being' (Oakeshott 1983: 25).

51 This is partly because, along with other critics of Hegel's position (such as Gadamer and Arthur Danto), Oakeshott stresses that an historical account will ultimately be formulated in response to particular historical questions, which will inevitably change with time. But he also stresses, rather more than the others, the relative paucity and elusive nature of the evidence we have to work with, hence rendering a complete account of the past all but impossible to give. For Hegel's views, see, in particular, Hegel (1980).

52 For this reason, Oakeshott seems to prefer Sir Ronald Syme's account of the changes occurring under Octavian in the last days of the Roman Republic to that given by Professor Hugh Last, since the former represents the changes 'in terms of the contingent transactions of assignable agents', whereas the latter explores them 'in terms of the modification of a practice'. See Oakeshott (1975: 100 n. 1). He stresses, however, that both are legitimate forms of historical investigation.

Chapter 3

1 'Abstract', 'concrete', 'experience' and 'world of ideas' are all examples of terms that have a particular Idealist-inspired meaning in this work, as we saw in the last chapter. See Chapter 2, section I for more details.

2 Furthermore, Oakeshott also uses the term 'contingent' in a highly idiosyncratic way both in *On Human Conduct* and in *On History*, as we saw in the last chapter – see section III, parts 1 and 3.

3 See the previous chapter for some of the ambiguities inherent in Oakeshott's notion of tradition and practice (particularly section II) and Raphael (1964) for further queries about what exactly Oakeshott means by terms like 'the self' and 'activity' – queries which Oakeshott largely ignores in his reply (Oakeshott 1965). (For Raphael's rejoinder, to the debate see Raphael [1965].)

4 Oakeshott does clarify somewhat what he means by 'practice' in his later work in Oakeshott (1975: 57 n.1). But even so, the term 'practice' is so all-embracing, that at the very least it invites a lot more discussion of the term than he provides.
5 There is some evidence that Oakeshott was interested in Arendt's work, in that he reviewed Arendt's *Between Past and Future* (Arendt 1961; Oakeshott 1962), and also drew upon her distinction between 'action' and 'fabrication' from *The Human Condition*, even if only to dispute it (Arendt 1958; Oakeshott 1975: 35–6). It is also possible that the very title of Oakeshott's *On Human Conduct* echoes that of Arendt's *The Human Condition* (Oakeshott 1975; Arendt 1958). For a comparison, see Canovan (1997). Oakeshott barely refers to the others, although some secondary authors have now begun to make some comparisons, including Franco (2003) and O'Sullivan (1999). The absence of a powerful book-length study comparing Oakeshott and Hayek is striking.
6 D. D. Raphael, for example, complained (in a not unsympathetic review of *On Human Conduct*) that when reading the work 'one is nonplussed by the wealth of assertion (and the still greater wealth of denial) with so little in the way of supporting grounds'. See Raphael (1975: 454).
7 The concept of a 'public intellectual' is one that has been particularly explored by Stefan Collini. See Collini (1991) and Collini (2006). For an appreciation, but also some queries of his approach, see Neill (2008).
8 Oakeshott certainly exerted a considerable – if sometimes subversive – influence on the way politics and political theory were studied through his lectures and seminars at the London School of Economics, which influenced a considerable number of academics teaching politics, among them Noel O'Sullivan, Nevil Johnson and David Boucher, to name but three. For Oakeshott's approach to politics – and its rivals, see Kenny (2004). To his contemporaries, Oakeshott was usually represented as an uncritical upholder of tradition. See for example, Benn and Peters (1959: 312–18).
9 See, for example, *Political Theory* 4/3 (1976), a special issue dedicated to analysing *On Human Conduct*, where – perhaps understandably due to the difficulty of the work – the contributors largely fail to understand Oakeshott's position. For a

more fruitful recent symposium on Oakeshott's work, see the *European Journal of Political Theory* 4 (2005).

10 This is not to suggest that this approach cannot also be insightful. See Podoksik (2005).

11 To label Mill's position in his *System of Logic* is somewhat controversial, since he specifically denies that his position is fully determinist, contrasting his argument with Robert Owen's. But in fact Mill's distinction seems unconvincing, as a number of commentators have noted. See Ryan (1987: 103–31.)

12 As W. H. Greenleaf amongst others has pointed out, both Weldon and Oakeshott consistently ignore the obvious point that if a philosopher succeeds in removing various traditional metaphysical justifications for actions in practice, then philosophizing will still have highly important practical implications, even if only in a negative sense, provided that such metaphysical justifications are still in vogue. Since this was certainly the case in post-war Britain, where a keen debate was being fought over whether the imposition of moral standards by law could be justified on a philosophical basis, this looks like almost wilful blindness. See Greenleaf (1968: 100).

13 Thus in particular, Weldon's justification for his argument that philosophy cannot provide justification for normative political arguments is much more linguistic than Oakeshott's. For Weldon, one of the fundamental mistakes committed by traditional political philosophers is their assumption that there is always an essential definition available for any given political concept – such as, for example, liberty or justice. But in fact, Weldon argued, such an assumption is quite wrong: the only way to discover the meaning of political concepts is through their use – and such uses are constantly changing. Since no philosophical technique can establish exactly what a given concept means in the first place, in other words, it is nonsensical to suggest that political philosophers will ever be able to advocate a particular conception of it as more laudable than another. See Weldon (1953: 28–9).

14 There are, however, some differences between Wittgenstein and Winch's positions. In particular, Winch is much keener to argue that some reflective ability is necessary to follow a rule intelligently than Wittgenstein is: the latter sometimes writes about rule-following as though it is a relatively automatic

process. See Winch (1958: 64–5). Furthermore, from the Wittgensteinian premise that all concepts presuppose social relations, it does not follow – as Winch seems to argue – that all social relations presuppose concepts, let alone that 'social relations between men exist only in and through their ideas' (Winch 1958: 123).

[15] For although the Thelemites were ostensibly simply following a particular Augustinian *precept* – namely 'love and do what you will' – Oakeshott stresses that they were in fact obeying the rules of conduct, the 'language of moral intercourse', into which they had been educated. The example of a monastic life is also used by Winch. See Winch (1958: 52).

[16] By contrast, Paul Ricoeur famously argues that psychoanalysis is a discipline that must combine both dialogic and causal approaches. See Ricoeur (1981).

[17] See Chapter 2, Section III, 1.

[18] See, for example, (Hegel 1977: section 653; 396): 'Language . . . only emerges as the middle term, mediating between independent and acknowledged self-consciousnesses; . . . the content of the language of conscience is the *self that knows itself as essential being.*'

[19] As Winch insists, 'the philosophical problems which arise there are not tiresome foreign bodies which must be removed before sociology can advance on its own independent scientific lines'. See Winch (1958: 42; more generally see 40–4).

[20] This charge is neatly summed up by Judith Shklar's description of Cold War liberalism as 'The Liberalism of Fear'. See Shklar (1989).

[21] Obviously this selection does not exhaust potential candidates to be 'Cold War liberals', even amongst prominent post-war thinkers – F. A. Hayek is just one other plausible candidate. However, as I argue below, there are good reasons to suggest that he (like Oakeshott) differs from the Cold War liberals on several important points. In general, my account of Cold War liberalism borrows heavily from an excellent article on the subject by Jan-Werner Muller. See Muller (2008). For a reading of Oakeshott and the others that concentrates more on examining their relationship with post-war positivism, see Neill (2009 – forthcoming).

22 See, for example, Crosland (1956) and Bell (2000). It is true that both of these texts are more concerned to prove that Marxism (rather than political ideas in general) had become redundant. But equally both took the value of technocratic welfare state capitalism as a given. In Crosland's case, this led him to take economic growth (and the desirability of the post-war British state) for granted when arguing for equality; in Bell's case it led him to reject the importance of non-economic arguments for equality – as evidenced by his subsequent splenetic dismissal of the value of the 'new social movements' of the 1960s. See Crosland (1956: 515) and Bell (2000: 425–33.)

23 As Muller notes, however, it is important to note that they all took Marx seriously, devoting considerable time to discussing his work. See, for example, Berlin (1939); Popper (1966, vol. 2) and Aron (1968, vol. 1).

24 The idea that mankind had a 'true' nature waiting to be discovered is a fallacy that has been widespread amongst Western political thinkers, Berlin believed, including Lenin, de Maistre, Lassalle, Locke and Burke as well as many others (Berlin 1964: 18–19). Ultimately this fallacy, Berlin believed, was related to a more fundamental mistake – namely that, underlying reality, there was some ultimate substance that philosophers could gain knowledge of, presumably by non-empirical means (Berlin 1999: 80). For more on the relationship between Berlin's more purely philosophical works and his ethical and political theory, see Reed (2008).

25 As Berlin puts it: 'If we ask the Kantian question, "In what kind of world is political philosophy – the kind of discussion and argument in which it consists – in principle possible?" the answer must be "Only in a world where ends collide".' See Berlin (1964: 8).

26 In Popper's formulation of the principle, that 'it must be the principle of all morality that no man should consider himself more valuable than any other person' (Popper 1966: vol. 1, 256–7, n. 20).

27 This ideal was explicitly linked to a British model of government and society by all three thinkers. For the importance of benign traditions, see, for example, Popper (2002).

28 Aron somewhat regretfully commented that he was 'personellement, keynesien avec quelque regret du liberalisme' (Aron 2002: 10). Popper's social democratic commitments are usefully highlighted in Magee (1985: 85, and passim).

Chapter 4

1 See Chapter 2 for some prominent examples of scholars who believe that Oakeshott should be classified as liberal, and equally for some who think Oakeshott should be classified as a conservative. More generally, while the literature on political ideologies is vast, particularly penetrating on the relationship between liberalism and conservatism are (Freeden 1996), especially chapters 8 and 9, and (Eatwell and O'Sullivan 1989), on the nature of the Right.

2 For a fuller analysis of the way that political ideologies altered during the course of the 19th century, see Neill (2006), an analysis I borrow from here.

3 Thus for Franco, what makes Oakeshott's arguments for 'liberalism' superior to (for example) Berlin's is that he is able to distinguish between legitimate and illegitimate forms of state intervention. For Berlin, in other words, any inference by the state must be considered a diminution of one's liberty; for Oakeshott, it very much depends upon the nature of the state intervention involved (see Franco 2003: 503). As far as it goes, this argument seems perfectly sound – but it does not of course do very much to prove Oakeshott's alleged 'liberalism'.

4 The sharp distinction that Oakeshott draws relatively late in his career – in 'The Masses in Representative Democracy' (1961) – between 'individuals' who are able to cope with modernity, and 'anti-individuals' who cannot, is one factor that should make us hesitate before considering Oakeshott's candidature as a 'liberal' political thinker. (See Oakeshott [1991: 363–83].) The vestiges of a more hierarchical conservatism do sometimes appear in Oakeshott's thought, even if they are not particularly significant in general in his later work.

Bibliography

Anonymous (1990), 'Editorial' *The Times* (22 November): 11.
Arendt, Hannah (1958), *The Human Condition*. Chicago: University of Chicago Press.
—(1961), *Between Past and Future: Six Exercises in Political Thought*. London: Faber and Faber.
Aron, Raymond (1961), 'La définition libérale de la liberté' *Archives Européennes de Sociologie* 2: 199–218.
—(1968), *Main Currents of Sociological Thought*, trans. Richard Howard and Helen Weaver, 2 vols. New York: Anchor Books.
—(1969), 'Liberté, liberale ou libertaire?' in Keba M'Baye, La liberte et l'ordre social: Textes des conferences et des entretiens organises par les Rencontres Internationales de Geneve. Neuchatel: Editions de la Baconniere, pp. 67–112.
—(2002), *L'Opium des Intellectuels*. Paris: Hachette Litterature.
Ayer, A. J. (1936), *Language, Truth and Logic*. London: Victor Gollancz.
—(1967), 'Man as a Subject for Science' in Peter Laslett and W. G. Runciman (eds), *Philosophy, Politics and Society: Third Series*. Oxford: Blackwell, pp. 6–24.
Bell, Daniel (2000), *The End of Ideology: On the Exhaustion of Political Ideas in the Fifties*, rev. edition. Cambridge, MA: Harvard University Press.
Benn, S. I. and Peters, R. S. (1959), *Social Principles and the Democratic State*. London: Allen and Unwin.
Bentham, Jeremy (1983), *Constitutional Code*, vol. 1, ed. Fred Rosen and J. H. Burns. Oxford: Clarendon Press.
Berlin, Isaiah (1939), *Karl Marx: His Life and Environment*. London: Thornton Butterworth.
—(1964), 'Does Political Theory Still Exist?' in Peter Laslett and W. G. Runciman (eds), *Philosophy, Politics and Society: Second Series*. Oxford: Blackwell.

—(1999), 'Logical Translation' in Isaiah Berlin, *Concepts and Categories: Philosophical Essays*, (ed.) Henry Hardy. London: Pimlico.
Bosanquet, Bernard (1912a), 'Introduction: The Central Experiences' in Bernard Bosanquet, *The Principle of Individuality and Value*. London: Macmillan.
—(1912b), 'The Concrete Universal' in Bernard Bosanquet, *The Principle of Individuality and Value*. London: Macmillan.
—(1923), *The Philosophical Theory of the State*, fourth edition. London: Macmillan.
Boucher, David (1984), 'The Creation of the Past: British Idealism and Michael Oakeshott's Philosophy of History' *History and Theory* 23: 193–214.
—(1991), 'Politics in a Different Mode: an Appreciation of Michael Oakeshott' *History of Political Thought* 7: 717–28.
—and Vincent, Andrew (2000), *British Idealism and Political Theory*. Edinburgh: Edinburgh University Press.
Bradley, F. H. (1914), 'Of Truth and Coherence' in F. H. Bradley, *Essays on Truth and Reality*. Oxford: Clarendon Press.
—(1922), *Principles of Logic*. London: Oxford University Press.
—(1968), *Appearance and Reality*, second revised edition. Oxford: Clarendon Press.
Bradley, John (1971), *Mach's Philosophy of Science*. London: Athlone Press.
Burke, Edmund (1826), *The Works of the Rt. Hon. Edmund Burke*. London: Printed for C. and J. Rivington, St Paul's Church-Yard and Waterloo-Place, Pall-Mall.
Canovan, Margaret (1997), 'Hannah Arendt as a Conservative Thinker' in Larry May and Jerome Kohn (eds), *Hannah Arendt: Twenty Years Later*. Cambridge, MA: MIT Press.
Coats, W. John (1985), 'Michael Oakeshott as Liberal Theorist' *Canadian Journal of Political Science* 18: 773–87.
Collingwood, R. G. (1924), *Speculum Mentis, or, The Map of Knowledge*. Oxford: Clarendon Press.
—(1934), 'Review of Michael Oakeshott, Experience and its Modes' *Cambridge Review* 55.
—(1938), *The Principles of Art*. Oxford: Clarendon Press.
Collini, Stefan (1991), *Public Moralists: Political Thought and Intellectual Life in Britain 1850–1930*. Oxford: Clarendon Press.

—(2006), *Absent Minds: Intellectuals in Britain.* Oxford: Oxford University Press.

Crick, Bernard (1963), 'The World of Michael Oakeshott or the Lonely Nihilist' *Encounter* 20: 65–7.

Crosland, C. A. R. (1956), *The Future of Socialism.* London: Jonathan Cape.

Crossman, Richard (1951), 'Review of Michael Oakeshott, *Political Education*' *New Statesman and Nation* 42: 60–1.

Dallmayr, Fred (1984), *Polis and Praxis: Exercises in Contemporary Political Theory.* Cambridge MA: MIT Press.

Danto, Arthur (1965), *Analytical Philosophy of History.* Cambridge: Cambridge University Press.

Devigne, Robert (1994), *Recasting Conservatism: Oakeshott, Strauss, and the Response to Postmodernism.* New Haven: Yale University Press.

Dray, W. H. (1968), 'Michael Oakeshott's Theory of History' in Preston King and B. C. Parekh (eds), *Politics and Experience: Essays Presented to Professor Michael Oakeshott on the Occasion of his Retirement.* Cambridge: Cambridge University Press, pp. 19–42.

Eatwell, Roger and O'Sullivan, Noel (eds) (1989), *The Nature of the Right: American and European Politics and Political Thought Since 1789.* London: Pinter Publishers.

Franco, Paul (1990a), 'Michael Oakeshott as Liberal Theorist' *Political Theory* 18: 411–36.

—(1990b), *The Political Philosophy of Michael Oakeshott.* New Haven: Yale University Press.

—(2003), 'Oakeshott, Berlin and Liberalism' *Political Theory* 31: 484–507.

—(2004), *Michael Oakeshott: An Introduction.* New Haven: Yale University Press.

Freeden, Michael (1996), *Ideologies and Political Theory.* Oxford: Clarendon Press.

Gadamer, Hans-Georg (1989), *Truth and Method*, second revised edition, trans. Joel Weinsheimer and Donald G. Marshall. London: Sheed and Ward.

Gallie, W. B. (1964), *Philosophy and Historical Understanding.* London: Chatto and Windus.

Gardiner, Patrick (1952), *The Nature of Historical Explanation*. London: Oxford University Press.

Gellner, Ernest (1995), 'Review of Ralf Dahrendorf, *LSE: A History of the London School of Economics and Political Science*' *Times Literary Supplement* (9 June): 3.

Gerencser, S. A. (2000), *The Skeptic's Oakeshott*. Basingstoke: Macmillan.

Grant, Robert (1990), *Oakeshott*. London: Claridge Press.

Gray, John (1993), *Post-liberalism: Studies in Political Thought*. New York: Routledge.

Greenleaf, W. H. (1966), *Oakeshott's Philosophical Politics*. London: Longmans.

—(1968), 'Idealism, Modern Philosophy and Politics' in Preston King and B. C. Parekh (eds), *Politics and Experience: Essays Presented to Professor Michale Oakeshott on the Occasion of his Retirement*. Cambridge: Cambridge University Press.

Hart, H. L. A. (1961), *The Concept of Law*. Oxford: Clarendon Press.

Hayek, F. A. (1960), *The Constitution of Liberty*. London: Routledge and Kegan Paul.

—(1973–79), *Law, Legislation and Liberty*, 3 vols. London: Routledge and Kegan Paul.

—(1978), *New Studies in Philosophy, Politics, Economics and the History of Ideas*. London: Routledge and Kegan Paul.

Hegel, G. W. F. (1952), *The Philosophy of Right*, trans. T. M. Knox. Oxford: Oxford University Press.

—(1977), *The Phenomenology of Spirit*, trans. A. V. Miller. Oxford: Clarendon Press.

—(1980), *Lectures on the Philosophy of World History*, trans. H. B. Nisbet. Cambridge: Cambridge University Press.

Hobhouse, L. T. (1991), *Liberalism*. London: Williams and Norgate.

Humboldt, Wilhelm von (1969), *The Limits of State Action*, ed. and trans. J. W. Burrow. Cambridge: Cambridge University Press.

Hylton, Peter (1990), *Russell, Idealism, and the Emergence of Analytic Philosophy*. Oxford: Clarendon Press.

Joachim, H. H. (1919), *Immediate Experience and Mediation*. Oxford: Clarendon Press.

Kelly, P. J. (1999), 'Contextual and Non-contextual Histories of Political Thought' in Jack Hayward, Brian Barry, and Archie

Brown (eds), *The British Study of Politics in the Twentieth Century.* Oxford: The British Academy, pp. 37–62.

Kelsen, Hans (1989), *Pure Theory of Law*, second edition, trans. Max Knight. Gloucester, MA: Peter Smith.

Kenny, Michael (2004), 'The Case for Disciplinary History: Political Studies in the 1950s and 1960s' *British Journal of Politics and International Relations* 6: 565–83.

King, Preston (1983), 'Michael Oakeshott and Historical Particularism' in Preston King (ed.), *The History of Ideas*. London: Croom Helm, pp. 96–132.

Koerner, Kirk (1985), *Liberalism and its Critics.* London: Croom Helm.

Laslett, Peter, ed. (1956), *Philosophy, Politics, and Society: A Collection.* Oxford: Blackwell.

Mach, Ernst (1914), *The Analysis of Sensations*, trans. C. M. Williams. London: Open Court.

Magee, Bryan (1985), *Popper.* London: Fontana Press.

McTaggart, J. McTaggart E. (1934), *Philosophical Studies*, ed. S. V. Keeling. London: Edward Arnold.

Meiland, J. W. (1965), *Scepticism and Historical Knowledge.* New York: Random House.

Minogue, Kenneth (1991), 'Michael Oakeshott and the History of Political Thought Seminar' *Cambridge Review* (October): 114–17.

Muller, Jan-Werner (2008), 'Fear and Freedom: On "Cold War liberals"' *European Journal of Political Theory* 7: 45–64.

Nardin, Terry (2001), *The Philosophy of Michael Oakeshott.* University Park, PA: Pennsylvania State University Press.

Neill, Edmund (2004), 'Review of *Roy Tseng, The Sceptical Idealist*' *English Historical Review* cxix (483): 1010–12.

—(2006), 'Political Ideologies: Liberalism, Conservatism, and Socialism' in Stefan Berger (ed.), *A Companion to Nineteenth-Century Europe, 1789–1914.* Oxford: Blackwell, pp. 211–23.

—(2008), 'Plus Ca Change: Some Criticisms of Stefan Collini's *Absent Minds*' *Political Studies Review* 6: 23–31.

—(forthcoming, 2012), 'The Impact of Positivism: Academic Political Thought in Britain, c. 1945–70' *History of European Ideas.*

Nietzsche, Friedrich (1994), *On the Genealogy of Morality*, ed. Keith Ansell-Pearson, trans. Carol Diethe. Cambridge: Cambridge University Press.

Oakeshott, Michael (1925), 'A Discussion of Some Matters Preliminary to the Study of Political Philosophy' LSE archives.
—(1933), *Experience and its Modes*. Cambridge: Cambridge University Press.
—(1937/8), 'Review of R. G. Collingwood, *The Principles of Art*' *Cambridge Review* 59.
—(1938), 'The Concept of a Philosophical Jurisprudence' *Politica* 3: 203–22; 345–60.
—ed. (1939), *The Social and Political Doctrines of Contemporary Europe*. New York: Cambridge University Press.
—(1960s), *The History of Political Thought from the Ancient Greeks to the Present Day*. Unpublished: LSE 1/1/21.
—(1962), 'Review of *Hannah Arendt: Between Past and Future: Six Exercises in Political Thought*' *Political Science Quarterly* 77: 88–90.
—(1965), 'A Reply to Professor Raphael' *Political Studies* 13: 89–92.
—(1975), *On Human Conduct*. Oxford: Clarendon Press.
—(1976), 'On Misunderstanding Human Conduct: A Reply to My Critics' *Political Theory* 4.
—(1983), *On History and Other Essays*. Oxford: Blackwell.
—(1991), *Rationalism in Politics and Other Essays*, revised edition. Indianapolis: Liberty Fund.
—(1993a), *Morality and Politics in Modern Europe*, ed. S. R. Letwin. New Haven: Yale University Press.
—(1993b), *Religion, Politics and the Moral Life*, ed. T. Fuller. New Haven: Yale University Press.
—(2000), *Hobbes on Civil Association*, revised edtion. Indianapolis: Liberty Fund.
—(2004), *What is History? And Other Essays*, ed. Luke O'Sullivan. Exeter: Imprint Academic.
—and Griffith, Guy (1936), *A Guide to the Classics, or How to Pick the Derby Winner*. London: Faber and Faber.
O'Sullivan, Luke (2000), 'Michael Oakeshott on European Political History' *History of Political Thought* 21: 132–51.
—(2003), *Oakeshott on History*. Exeter: Imprint Academic.
O'Sullivan, Noel (1999), 'Visions of Freedom: The Response to Totalitarianism' in Jack Hayward, Brian Barry and Archie Brown (eds), *The British Study of Politics in the Twentieth Century*. Oxford: British Academy, pp. 63–88.

Pitkin, Hanna F. (1973), 'The Roots of Conservatism: Michael Oakeshott and the Denial of Politics' *Dissent* 20: 496–525.

Podoksik, Efraim (2003), *In Defence of Modernity: Vision and Philosophy in Michael Oakeshott*. Exeter: Imprint Academic.

—(2005), 'How Oakeshott Became an Oakeshottian' *European Journal of Political Theory* 4: 67–88.

Polanyi, Michael (1958), *Personal Knowledge: Towards a Post-Critical Philosophy*. London: Routledge and Kegan Paul.

Popper, Karl (1957), *The Poverty of Historicism*. London: Routledge and Kegan Paul.

—(1966), *The Open Society and its Enemies*, 2 vols. London: Routledge and Kegan Paul.

—(2002), 'Towards a Rational Theory of Tradition' in Karl Popper, *Conjectures and Refutations: The Growth of Scientific Knowledge*, third edition. London: Routledge, pp. 161–82.

Price, Russell (1991), 'Memories of Michael Oakeshott' *Cambridge Review* (October): 117–20.

Quinton, Anthony (1971), 'Absolute Idealism' *Proceedings of the British Academy* 58: 303–29.

Raphael, D. D. (1964), 'Professor Oakeshott's *Rationalism in Politics*' *Political Studies* 12: 202–15.

—(1965), '*Rationalism in Politics*. A Note on Professor Oakeshott's Reply' *Political Studies* 13: 395–7.

—(1975), 'Review of *On Human Conduct*' *The Political Quarterly* 46: 450, 452, 454.

Rawls, John (1971), *A Theory of Justice*. Oxford: Oxford University Press.

—(1995), *Political Liberalism*, revised edition. New York: Columbia University Press.

—(1999), 'The Idea of Public Reason Revisited' in John Rawls, (ed.) *The Law of Peoples*. Cambridge MA: Harvard University Press.

Raz, Joseph (1986), *The Morality of Freedom*. Oxford: Clarendon Press.

Reed, Jamie (2008), 'From Logical Positivism to "Metaphysical Rationalism": Isaiah Berlin on the "Fallacy of Reduction"' *History of Political Thought* 28: 109–31.

Ricoeur, Paul (1981), 'The Question of Proof in Freud's Psychoanalytic Writings' in Paul Ricoeur, *Hermeneutics and the Human*

Sciences, ed. and trans. John B. Thompson. Cambridge: Cambridge University Press, pp. 247–73.

Riley, Patrick (1991), 'Michael Oakeshott, Political Philosopher' *Cambridge Review* (October): 110–13.

Rorty, Richard (1980), *Philosophy and the Mirror of Nature*. Oxford: Blackwell.

Rotenstreich, Nathan (1976), *Philosophy, History and Politics: Studies in Contemporary English Philosophy of History*. The Hague: Martinus Nijhoff.

Ryan, Alan (1987), *The Philosophy of John Stuart Mill*. Basingstoke: Macmillan.

Ryle, Gilbert (1949), *The Concept of Mind*. London: Hutchinson.

Shklar, Judith (1989), 'The Liberalism of Fear' in Nancy L. Rosenblum (ed.), *Liberalism and the Moral Life*. Cambridge, MA: Harvard University Press.

Spencer, Herbert (1909), *The Man Versus the State*. London: Watts.

Strauss, Leo (1953), *Natural Right and History*. Chicago: University of Chicago Press.

—(1959), *What is Political Philosophy? And Other Studies*. Glencoe: Free Press.

Tocqueville, Alexis de (1861), Memoir, Letters, and Remains of Alexis de Tocqueville, vol. 1. Cambridge: Macmillan.

Tregenza, Ian (2003), *Michael Oakeshott on Hobbes: A Study in the Renewal of Philosophical Ideas*. Exeter: Imprint Academic.

Tseng, Roy (2003), *The Sceptical Idealist: Michael Oakeshott as a Critic of Enlightenment*. Thorverton: Imprint Academic.

Walsh, W. H. (1968), 'The Practical and Historical Past' in Preston King and B. C. Parekh (eds), *Politics and Experience: Essays Presented to Professor Michael Oakeshott on the Occasion of his Retirement*. Cambridge: Cambridge University Press, pp. 5–18.

Weber, Max (1968), *Economy and Society: An Outline of Interpretive Sociology*, 3 vols. New York: Bedminster Press.

—(1994), *Political Writings*, ed. Peter Lassman and Ronald Speirs. Cambridge: Cambridge University Press.

Weldon, T. D. (1953), *The Vocabulary of Politics*. Harmondsworth: Penguin Books.

Winch, Peter (1958), *The Idea of a Social Science and its Relation to Philosophy*. London: Routledge and Kegan Paul.

Wittgenstein, Ludwig (1961), *Tractatus Logico-Philosophicus*, ed. A. J. Ayer, trans. D. F. Pears and B. F. McGuinness. London: Routledge and Kegan Paul.

Worthington, Glenn (1995), 'Michael Oakeshott on Life: Waiting with Godot' *History of Political Thought* 16: 59–68.

—(2000), 'Michael Oakeshott and the City of God', *Political Theory* 28: 377–98.

Index

Acton, Lord 4
anthropology 27–8
Arendt, Hannah 46, 80, 99, 124
Aristotle 8, 57, 58, 59, 60, 80, 88, 99, 121
Arnold, Matthew 8
Aron, Raymond 90–5, 127
Augustine, Saint 9
Ayer, A. J. 12, 84, 91

Bacon, Francis 12, 39–40, 80, 118
Barker, Ernest 35
Bell, Daniel 127
Bentham, Jeremy 101
Berlin, Isaiah 80, 90–6, 112, 127, 128
Bosanquet, Bernard 18, 20, 116, 117
Boucher, David 124
Bradley, F. H. 6, 18, 19, 20, 21, 23, 116, 117–18
Burckhardt, Jacob 5
Burke, Edmund 106, 127

Cambridge 4–7
Cambridge Journal 7, 37
Carlyle, Thomas 106
Caruso, Enrico 10
Cecil, Lord Hugh 107
Charvet, John 9
Chaucer 87
chemistry 54

civil association 14, 61–7, 96, 109, 110, 121, 122
Collingwood, R. G. 11, 12, 36, 81–3, 95, 97, 117, 118, 122
Collini, Stefan 124
communism 35, 37
'Concept of a Philosophical Jurisprudence, The' 33
conservatism 2, 14, 15, 99, 105–8, 109–13, 116, 128
Constant, Benjamin 101, 102, 103
corruption of consciousness 36, 118
Cranston, Maurice 9
Crick, Bernard 2
Croce, Benedetto 18
Crosland, C. A. R. 127
Crossman, Richard 1, 2

Danto, Arthur 115, 122
Descartes, Rene 12, 39–40, 80
Dicey, A. V. 4
'Discussion of Some Matters Preliminary to the Study of Political Philosophy, A' 20
Durkheim, Emile 87

economics 27–8, 29, 108
Engels, Friedrich 41
Enlightenment 12, 16, 17, 32, 33, 38, 39, 46, 73, 77, 99, 100, 105, 111, 119

Index

enterprise association 62–3, 65
ethics 24, 35, 54
European Economic Community 81
Experience and Its Modes 6, 13, 14, 17, 20–31, 32–5, 36, 37, 42, 49–51, 53–4, 79, 80, 81–2, 97, 118, 119, 120, 122

fabrication 124
Foucault, Michel 99
Franco, Paul 110, 113, 128
freedom *see* liberty
Freeden, Michael 108
French Revolution 100, 105
Freud, Sigmund 88

Gadamer, Hans-Georg 99, 121, 122
Gallie, W. B. 115
Gardiner, Patrick 115
Gellner, Ernest 1
Gentile, Giovanni 18
Gierke, Otto von 121
Grant, Rev. Cecil 4
Gray, John 116
Green, T. H. 18
Greenleaf, W. H. 125
Guide to the Classics, or How to Pick the Derby Winner, A 6

Habermas, Jurgen 99
Hart, H. L. A. 96, 122
Hayek, F. A. 1, 40, 80, 93, 94, 95, 96, 104, 109, 110, 112, 113, 124, 126
Hegel, G. W. F. 4, 20, 63, 70, 71, 89, 102, 122, 123, 126
Heidegger, Martin 5, 122
history 2, 4, 5, 8, 11, 12, 14–15, 17, 23, 24, 33, 52, 69–77, 81–2, 91–2, 98, 99, 117, 122
as a mode *see* modes

philosophy of 11, 14, 17, 69–77, 98
of political thought 4, 8, 99
'History of Political Thought from the Ancient Greeks to the Present Day, The' 8
Hobbes, Thomas 32, 47, 96, 98, 119, 120, 121, 122
Hobhouse, L. T. 103
Hobson, J. A. 103
Holderlin, Friedrich 5
human conduct 12, 13, 52, 54–61, 69–72, 83, 86, 90, 94, 97
Humboldt, Wilhelm von 101
Hume, David 18

Idealism 4, 6, 13, 17–24, 32, 34, 79, 80, 81–3, 84, 89, 123
individuality 4, 11, 16, 17, 19–20, 31, 32, 33, 47–9, 51–2, 53, 55–6, 59–61, 62–5, 66, 72, 78, 79, 82–3, 92–6, 99–105, 105–6, 108–9, 109–13, 115, 128
and conservatism 105–6, 108–9, 110–13
historical theorising of 69–77
and Idealism 19–20
and liberalism 92–6, 99–105, 108–9, 110–13
modern pluralist 4, 11, 14, 16, 33, 47–9, 52, 53, 59–61, 62–5, 66, 78, 79, 82–3, 92–6, 128

Joachim, Harold 116
Johnson, Nevil 2, 124
jurisprudence 33–4, 54
justice 67, 92, 94, 115

Kant, Immanuel 4, 47, 93, 94, 95, 104, 115, 127
Kedourie, Elie 9
Kelsen, Hans 122
Kidd, Benjamin 107

Index

Laski, Harold 1, 7, 80
Lassalle, Ferdinand 127
Last, Hugh 123
law 34, 44, 46, 49, 62, 63–4, 66–9, 71, 77, 78, 96, 101, 104, 110, 122, 125
  causal 26, 55, 71
  in civil association 63–9, 122
  Idealist theory of 33–4
  natural 46, 68
  rule of 49, 62, 78, 104
Lenin, V. I. 127
Letwin, Shirley Robin 9
liberalism 13, 14, 35, 83, 90–7, 98, 100–5, 106, 109–13, 115, 126, 128
  Cold War 83, 90–7, 104, 112, 126
liberty (or "freedom") 14, 31, 42, 56, 63, 66–7, 78, 79, 83, 92, 94, 96, 100–5, 105–8, 110–13, 119, 125, 128
Locke, John 41, 89, 127
London School of Economics 8

Mach, Ernst 84
Machiavelli, Niccolo 41
Maistre, Joseph de 106, 127
Maitland, F. W. 4
Mannheim, Karl 7
Marx, Karl 41, 91–2, 127
McTaggart, J. M. E. 4, 5
Mill, J. S. 18, 84, 101, 110, 125
Minogue, Kenneth 2, 9
modernity 15, 16, 29, 32–3, 46, 48, 51, 52, 59–60, 61, 63, 69, 77–8, 79, 82–3, 91–7, 99, 102–5, 106, 110–13, 116, 128
modes 13, 14, 22–31, 32, 33, 34, 49, 51, 53, 54, 70, 77, 78, 81–2, 84, 89, 97, 117
  differs from R. G. Collingwood 23, 81–3

  differs from Idealists 21–4
  History 69–77
  Poetry 33, 49–51
  Practice 28–31
  Science 24–8
Montaigne, Michel de 3, 9, 47
Montessori, Maria 4
morality
  and Aristotle 58–60
  of the common good 16, 47
  ideals and rules of 41, 42, 47–8, 57, 64, 66
  of individualism 16
  and language 58–60, 126
  and law 68–9, 125,
  pluralism 60, 91, 102–4, 109
  practices *see* practice
  pre-modern 16
Morality and Politics in Modern Europe 8, 47
Muller, Jan-Werner 126, 127

Nardin, Terry 15, 116
Nazism 37
Nietzsche, Friedrich 5, 107, 111
Nozick, Robert 113

On History and Other Essays 9, 14, 17, 69–77, 79, 123
On Human Conduct 3, 8, 9, 14, 17, 31, 33, 47, 49, 51–69, 78, 79, 80, 86, 111, 123, 124
orders of inquiry 54
O'Sullivan, Noel 2, 124
Owen, Robert 125

philosophy 1, 4, 5, 6, 10, 11, 13, 14, 16, 17, 20, 23–4, 29, 31–3, 34, 35, 49, 53, 54, 69, 81, 84–6, 89, 94, 97, 98, 115, 125
  of history *see* history

philosophy (*Cont'd*)
    and modes 21–4, 29, 31–3, 35, 49, 81, 97
    political 1, 35, 94, 115
phronesis 58–60, 121
physics 25–6, 54
Plato 8, 16
pluralism 17, 46, 49, 60, 77, 83, 91–2, 95–7, 102–6, 109
Podoksik, Efraim 15, 110, 112, 116
poetry *see* modes
Polanyi, Michael 12, 43
Popper, Karl 90–2, 94–5, 115, 127, 128
positivism 6, 12, 24, 25, 68, 84–6, 90–1, 94, 98, 126
    in post-war British philosophy 6, 12, 83–6
    in "Science", 24–7, 98
practical knowledge *see* practice
practice 12, 13, 16, 17, 22, 23, 24, 28–31, 32, 33, 35, 36, 37, 38–9, 43–5, 48, 49, 52, 53–4, 56–8, 64–5, 67, 69, 72, 77, 80, 85–6, 86–7, 89, 90, 97, 109, 118, 120–1, 123
    knowledge found in 38–9, 43, 44, 118
    as a mode *see* modes
    moral 57–8, 62, 64–5, 67, 109
    prudential 57
    and theory (or philosophy) 13, 16, 17, 23, 24, 35, 36, 53, 82, 85–6, 89, 97
Price, Russell 8
psychology 27–8, 54

Ranke, Leopold von 4
Raphael, D. D. 123, 124
rationalism 7, 12, 16, 17, 33, 37, 38–42, 46

Rationalism in Politics and Other Essays 8, 9, 14, 17, 31, 37–51, 57, 79, 80, 111, 118, 122
Rawls, John 13, 104, 105, 109, 115–16
Raz, Joseph 105
religion 3, 5, 15, 23, 30–1, 61, 82, 107, 117
respublica 80, 122
Ricoeur, Paul 126
Ryle, Gilbert 12, 43–4, 121

self-disclosure 60–1, 80
self-enactment 60–1
Shaw, George Bernard 3
Shelley, Percy Bysshe 50
Shklar, Judith 126
Social and Political Doctrines of Contemporary Europe, The 6
social Darwinism 107
social sciences 27, 86
sociology 86, 126
Spencer, Herbert 84, 107
Spinoza, Baruch 47, 80
Strauss, Leo 15, 46, 91, 95, 111
Stubbs, Bishop William 4
Syme, Sir Ronald 123

technical knowledge 32, 39, 41–3, 44, 118–19
Thatcher, Margaret 1, 108
Tocqueville, Alexis de 101, 102, 103
tradition 1–2, 7, 14, 16, 17–18, 24, 33, 35, 37–48, 56–7, 60–1, 72, 78, 79, 80, 88, 93, 95–6, 99, 101, 103, 104, 106, 107, 108, 109–10, 111, 112–13, 119, 120, 123, 124, 127
    British Idealist 17–18
    and knowledge 1–2, 7, 14, 37–48, 60–1, 88, 124

liberal 101, 103, 109–10, 112
  and pluralism 16, 17, 78, 95
  and practices 56–7, 72,
    120, 123
  Western European 35, 45–8,
    80, 95–6, 106, 107, 111, 119
Trietschke, Heinrich von 107
Tseng, Roy 15, 116

utilitarian 50, 92, 95, 99, 101, 115

Voegelin, Eric 46

Wallas, Graham 7
Weber, Max 27, 91, 95, 103–4, 120
Weldon, T. D. 12, 84–6, 89, 91,
  97, 125
welfare state 91, 94, 127
Whigs 102
Winch, Peter 86–90, 97, 125, 126
Wittgenstein, Ludwig 44, 86, 89, 125
Wordsworth, William 50
World War One 4, 10
World War Two 6, 10, 37, 38,
  107, 108, 112

www.ingramcontent.com/pod-product-compliance
Lightning Source LLC
Chambersburg PA
CBHW052050300426
44117CB00012B/2061